W9-CNO-430

A Servant's Manual

Other titles in

PRISMS

A Servant's Manual

Christian Leadership for Tomorrow

Michael W. Foss

FORTRESS PRESS

MINNEAPOLIS

A SERVANT'S MANUAL
Christian Leadership for Tomorrow

Copyright © 2002 Augsburg Fortress. All rights reserved. Except for brief quotations in critical articles or reviews, no part of this book may be reproduced in any manner without prior written permission from the publisher. Write: Permissions, Augsburg Fortress, Box 1209, Minneapolis, MN 55440.

Scripture quotations from the New Revised Standard Version of the Bible are copyright © 1989 by the Division of Christian Education of the National Council of the Churches of Christ in the United States of America and are used by permission.

Cover image: Copyright © José Ortega/Images.com. Used by permission.
Cover design: Kevin van der Leek Design Inc.
Book design and typesetting: Peregrine Graphics Services

Library of Congress Cataloging-in-Publication Data
Foss, Michael W.
   A servant's manual : Christian leadership for tomorrow / Michael W. Foss.
       p. cm.
   ISBN 0-8006-3453-5 (alk. paper)
      1. Pastoral theology. 2. Christian leadership.   I. Title.

BV4011.3 .F67 2002
253—dc21   2002021098

The paper used in this publication meets the minimum requirements of American National Standard for Information Sciences—Permanence of Paper for Printed Library Materials, ANSI Z329.48-1984.

Manufactured in the U.S.A.
06   05   04   03   02   1   2   3   4   5   6   7   8   9   10

Contents

Preface

Today's Christian leaders are stuck. Their ministries are being sapped of vital energy by endless controversy and lack of vision. Often leaders face crucial questions about church life and mission with alternatives that seem mutually exclusive or simply inadequate. In this little book I hope to offer a new style of thinking, one that can energize a new generation of Christian leaders.

I believe that the way through the church's present anemia lies in a new way of seeing that will no longer be stuck in false polarities and dead-end thinking. Spirit-led vision is required. This new insight will take seriously the demands of both the gospel and of our changing cultural context. It dares to believe that in the creative tension of faith-inspired thought the Holy Spirit is at work, renewing the Christian message for a new age—the twenty-first century.

My intent is to engage the reader in a hope-filled conversation. The vast sweep of cultural change provides the context of this book, while the sweeping claims of Jesus Christ set our course like a compass. In the tension of these two realities, the Christian leader is called to live, reflect, and witness. Although the call of faith is never easy, its fundamental imperatives must be rethought in light of and for the sake of the world.

The invitation to discipleship entails direct engagement with the world for which Jesus came, died, and was raised to new life.

There are no easy answers. There are, however, great possibilities. Such possibilities can only emerge as we discard old ways of thinking and embrace the inherent openness of our faith. Jesus models such thinking for us. Time and again he refused to get stuck in the either/or questions that would snare him in controversies going nowhere. His answer to the question of taxation is just one example. The Savior looked outside the question, thought beyond the given assumptions, and danced just outside their grasp.

Christians are called to do the same in our time. It will take courage and persistence. But we can do it.

Using models from contemporary science, I propose that the Spirit-led vision takes us beyond accepted polarities. Rather than accepting old dichotomies or making choices that confine the spirit of the gospel, I propose that we dance outside of them and ask how these polarities actually inform and shape one another. More than that, I propose that we anticipate where they might be leading us. Polarities may in fact represent two opposite points on a loop or spiral. The Christian leader is invited to recognize this possibility and then to "skate ahead" to a new place where we can respond freely and joyfully in faith. I hope this book will sketch the implications of this vision in workable ways for Christian leadership, worship, mission, and ministry.

A book like this is never the creation of one mind. Rather, it is the outcome of countless conversations with those who, as ordained and non-ordained leaders of the church, respond to the call to serve in Jesus' name. My thanks go to the staff and disciples gathered and scattered at Prince of Peace Lutheran Church in Burnsville, Minnesota. I continue to learn from them and with them. Especially I am grateful for the ongoing creativity of Handt Hanson and Alan Bachman, who model the "looping" of reality in their ministries as worship leader and administrative leader.

Thank you to Fortress Press, to Marv Roloff for the invitation to write this book, and to Hal Rast for serving as editor during a difficult time in his life.

This book is dedicated to Mark Zipper:
friend and fellow disciple who has encouraged
and challenged me to not just think outside the box
but to redraw the box.

1.
What's the Point?

One of the great accomplishments of the last century is the completion of the Human Genome Project, which set about to identify and map human DNA. The completion of this project raises specters of scientific Frankensteins rampaging out of control, as well as genetic alterations to avoid such genetic time bombs as heart disease and Huntington's disease.

Out of this research has emerged a picture of the workings of life itself. DNA does not exist in a straight line. It loops. The two strands of proteins loop around each other. This property makes possible the wonder of life: reproduction and mutation. At its core, life doesn't move in straight lines—*life loops!*

Christians who want to understand our time and circumstances in order to be effective in mission will understand that all of life loops. Straight-line thinking no longer works. There is no straight line between cause and effect in real life. The clash between faith and culture is often faith's desire for simple answers to complex phenomena. Or, to say it another way, it is straight-line response to

1

looping reality. No wonder Christian leaders are often left confused and dispirited. In contrast, we need to see life as a marvelous series of loops in which ministry can be powerful and productive.

"Hi, Pastor," she said with a smile. I had thought that I recognized her as I stepped up to the buffet line, but I couldn't put a name to the face.

"We just worshiped with you," she continued. "My daughter just became a new disciple at your church." She pointed to where two young people and an older man were sitting and eating. "It was wonderful. So thank you."

After I had eaten, I went to greet the four of them. That's when the young man smiled and said, "Thank you so much for all you do in the church. Sharon is coming to church again for the first time in over nine years."

Sharon smiled and said simply, "Your church has changed my life. I wouldn't miss it. Things just make a lot more sense now than before. . . . My life makes more sense."

And the family beamed.

In a time of great change, spiritual leaders often wonder, "What's the point?" What's the point of working so hard when the rewards seem so tenuous? What's the point when my ego is so often on the line—the criticisms are frequently loud, and the praise faint? What's the point when I don't see any of the fruits that tell me real people are meeting a real savior?

The point is discipleship: a spiritual transformation that leads to confident followership of Jesus Christ. The point is to equip more and more women and men, young people, children, and families with the confidence for life that Sharon now had. The point is to lift up the eternal truths and promises of God with the confidence of those who have seen and heard the witness of countless others—just like that young woman. The point is that no other organization besides the church can so effectively address the spiritual dimension of life for our world. We have the Word of God. We have the practices of spirituality that have stood the test of time. We have the necessary dual focus of the individual and the community. We are the point of intersection between faith and the world, between mortality and immortality. The church ought to be where the loops of life intersect with the power of the Spirit in a wonderful creative tension.

For every person critical of the church there are countless others who reap the rewards of discipleship through changed lives. They experience the reward of faith not only when death draws near, but also when hard decisions must be made. The power of transformed lives is evident when men or women walk away from the temptation of an extramarital affair because they know it goes against all they believe. The strength of a living faith is evident when young people refuse to cheat on a test—even though that test is a critical part of their grade and they haven't studied as hard as they might have. When businesspeople, professionals in countless fields, homemakers and stay-at-home dads make the daily decisions to reflect the one in whom they believe, the purpose of the church is made present in the real-life loops of our time.

Such interaction is creative. As the world loops into new and old forms, faith responds in mission. This response is creative and life-giving. The church's response through new forms invited Sharon back—and changed her life. Sharon is now a part of our church's looping in witness to the world; she will touch lives that previously have been unavailable to the Christian mission of the church. Sharon is the church splitting, like spiritual DNA, and growing into brand-new fields of hope and faith. Such "mutation" fulfills the command of Christ to "go, therefore, and make disciples of all nations, baptizing them in the name of the Father, and of the Son, and of the Holy Spirit, and teaching them to obey everything that I have commanded you" (Matthew 28:19-20).

From Doctrine to Experience to Biblical Literacy
(LOOP #1: THE CHURCH'S PATH)

There was a time when the point of ministry and church was clear. We lived in a denominationally relevant and defined world. Lutherans knew who they were in contrast to Baptists, Episcopalians, and Presbyterians. Doctrine—that specific slant on theology that existed within a particular denomination—was at the front door of our churches. It was so much more than whether we "believed in the pope" or baptized infants or only professed persons of "the age of discernment." Doctrine provided the clear boundaries within which we ministered. We taught our young and preached to our adults that our particular perspective on the Bible not only was true, but provided a spiritual advantage—if not before God, then at least in the confidence of our own souls.

I was serving a Lutheran congregation in Oregon when he walked into my office. He had a beard, and I hadn't seen him in a couple of years. I didn't recognize him. After we both got over that shock, he told me that he had left the Baptist ministry and wanted to join our Lutheran congregation.

"Do you really know what you are doing?" I asked him. "We believe in two sacraments. In the Lord's Supper, for example, we believe that Jesus is truly present—in, with, and under the bread and wine. We don't believe, like you Baptists, that we only think about Jesus when we share the Lord's Supper."

I have never forgotten his response. "Mike," he said, "I don't know a single Baptist pastor who believes what you just said we believe."

It wasn't just a challenge to my doctrinal assumptions. My theological arrogance, my sacramental superiority lay in shambles, and he explained to me his theology of the Lord's Supper. And it was *almost Lutheran!*

As the denominational walls have collapsed, we have listened to one another in Christ's church. We have discovered that we love the same savior, that we share some basic understandings of God's love, and that we even can disagree without being disagreeable.

Those of us within the church—pastors, staff, and lay leaders—are often the last ones to get it. We work within our particular frameworks of perspective only to be shocked when the world disconnects from us or has moved beyond us. So we get stuck—not because we do not care, nor because we are not willing to learn. It is rather that the language, activities, and symbols of our world presuppose a time and place that have passed.

What we need is a new way of thinking that can move us through the false dichotomies of our age and into this rich new world.

Nobel prize–winning physicist Richard Feynman, widely acclaimed for his extraordinary genius, had an I.Q. of only 122. Michael Michalko, in an article entitled "Thinking like a Genius," writes: "Whenever Feynman was stuck on a problem, he would invent new thinking strategies. He felt the secret to his genius was *his ability to disregard how past thinkers thought about problems and, instead, invent new ways to think.* He was so unstuck that if something didn't work he would look at it several different ways until he found a way that moved his imagination."[1]

Michalko suggests that such thinking is "productive thinking" as opposed to "reproductive thinking." Reproductive thinking reproduces the way we have previously thought about and approached problems. Not surprisingly, the solutions are almost always the same as have been suggested before. Productive thinking produces answers that are new because they spring from new strategies, new approaches. Michalko, along with Feynman and others, believes that we can learn this way of thinking.

In other words, it doesn't take a membership in Mensa or an I.Q. of 185 to think out of the box. Feynman's productive thinking can be practiced. Einstein's genius of bringing seeming opposites together can be learned. New thinking strategies can be developed, but only if we are willing to look beyond the already accepted categories and methods.

For the sake of spiritual transformation, leaders in the Christian church must learn to think "productively." Let us explore beyond the accepted definitions of our time. Let us not assume that our inherited definitions and dichotomies must necessarily stand forever—for the sake of engaging the world in the name of Jesus Christ. Productive thinking is a creative way of exploring the tension between the polarities, a dance with seeming opposites.

For example, the world has moved beyond doctrine to *experience.* My colleague and friend taught me a lesson that was a spiritual wake-up call. He was interested in our church not because of what we taught as doctrine but because of the God he experienced in worship, adult education classes, and our men's group.

Every week, millions of adults, teens, and children come to our churches. They have become less and less interested in first knowing our particular slant on the Trinity, baptism, or worship. They have come *hoping to meet God.* They have come for the healing of Christ's hand, the strengthening of the Holy Spirit's presence, and the hope of the promises of our creator God. They have come hoping to experience the results of an encounter with the divine, not just talk about the divine. They come looking for a real faith that works in their real lives—a faith that helps them make sense of their real world.

Being "talking heads" no longer cuts it. Rather, the biblical oneness of the self has emerged. It is not that the head should not be engaged. Rather, it is that the heart and the head—the whole self—must be invited into and then addressed in our churches. This is the transformation with which the first century caught fire.

St. Paul writes: "So if anyone is in Christ, there is a new creation: everything old has passed away; see, everything has become new" (2 Corinthians 5:17).

Every church seeks to provide an experience with the living God. The question is not whether we are doing so, but whether we are doing it with purpose and whether we expect changed lives to result from it.

■□■□■

"How am I going to provide an experience of worship? I serve in a small rural church. There is no way I can give my congregation what you at Prince of Peace give." I was leading a conversation with two hundred pastors from many denominations. This pastor knew of Prince of Peace—our worship and size. How could he translate what I was teaching into his own context?

"I am not suggesting that you give them the same experience we give," I answered. "And I don't believe that you don't already provide an experience for those who attend your church. Of course you do, that's why they keep coming. You provide an experience that fits their lives, with ritual and fellowship they understand. Watch and see how they greet one another; sit in the same pews, and stay to talk afterward. That is all part of a particular experience. The question I want to ask you to think about is this: Can this experience reach out to other generations, those outside the church, or not? If it can't, are you willing to craft another experience alongside of the one you provide now?"

"But," he persisted, "worship isn't entertainment."

"Experience and entertainment are not the same thing," I replied. "In fact, they are two different things. Real experience, especially true worship experience, must be much more than mere entertainment."

Experience versus Entertainment

Ministry as experience is separate from ministry as entertainment. Entertainment engages the person but does not expect a transformation. Experience, on the other hand, always results in a changed person. When we have experienced something, our worldview has been altered and our perspective on life has shifted. We can no longer see ourselves, God, or the world in the same way.

In their book *The Experience Economy*, James Gilmore and Joseph Pine help us understand both the nature of experience and how we have moved into an entire economy of experience.[2] They tell us that experience engages the whole person, while entertainment engages only the sensory self. The mind is fully engaged in experience, but not in entertainment. The consequence is that experience is the driving force of our economy. People strongly desire to be fully engaged. "Experience is a distinct form of economic output. Simultaneously, we are economizing our time and money. Yet, we are spending more and more money for experiences."[3]

Experience is the cultural key to meaning. One example of this that Gilmore and Pine address is the "American Girl Place" in Chicago. Young girls and their moms travel from across the United States to visit, have tea, watch a revue, and sing "The American Girl Anthem." This is an experience in identity, an experience in a particular culture in which the entire person is fully engaged. Gilmore and Pine speak of watching girls weep as they sing the anthem. Part of this experience, of course, is the sale of American Girl paraphernalia. But the goods purchased are investments in the memory of the experience.

Reproductive thinking would immediately assume that we must make a choice, then, between becoming entertaining or keeping biblical depth and fidelity. Reproductive thinking would tend to reassert doctrinal clarity over against experience as a key for meaning. Productive thinking, however, would look for a new strategy that could bring this seeming dichotomy (loop!) into a creative tension to better serve God's world through the gospel.

Productive thinking would assert that experience as an essential element of ministry does not mean that theology or doctrine has no place in our churches. Of course they do. In fact, I would argue that the need for solid biblical understanding is reinforced by effective experiences of God's presence. When people encounter the living God in worship or through another aspect of our ministries, they hunger to know the God they have met. This inner urge to "know God" is what doctrine or theology addresses. Experience, by itself, is like a river without banks. We call that a flood. Conversely, doctrine without experience is like the banks of a river without any water. We call that a drought.

The Bridge between Doctrine and Experience

Between experience and doctrine stands the Word. Biblical literacy is the bridge between an experience of the presence of God and our understanding of the God who alone is God. Thus, spiritual transformation (discipleship) is for a life of faith established upon the Word of God. The authority of the church was, at one time, sufficient to trumpet the right and wrong of any particular

theological position. In our postinstitutional world, however, that authority has eroded in our churches just as
surely as it has in other areas of society. (I will address
this more specifically in chapter 2.) The consequence is
that we must reestablish our credibility. The Bible is still
the most widely understood and respected source of spiritual authority in our world. In the United States, 80 percent of adults surveyed "regard the Bible as inspired
scripture."[4] This is not, however, a literalist view of the
Bible. In 1998, 33 percent of adults surveyed held the
Bible to be "literally true."[5] Nevertheless, "seventy-six
percent of the nation says that reading the Bible helps
them commune to a greater extent with God. Adults also
cite the feeling of peace and finding meaning in life as
primary benefits of reading Scripture."[6] When the Bible is
the source of our authority, we speak to some of the deepest spiritual impulses within people.

Experience becomes an open door for people to enter
into the presence of the revealed God of Scripture. The
Word grounds that experience in human history—the
Old Testament as the history of God's people before
Christ, and the New Testament as the historic meeting of
humanity with God in Christ. Doctrine becomes a doorway into deeper reflection on the character and activity
of this God we have come to experience and know.

Now that's productive thinking! And that is where this
postmodern world meets the historic confession of faith
in the witness of the church.

■□◧□■

"Well, Pastor Mike," she said with a smile. "I came to see
you because of a problem I have with the Bible. I love

Prince of Peace. God has changed my life here. And I am trying to be a disciple of Jesus Christ, so I lead a Bible study. But in this study it talks about predestination . . . and I don't get it. Why would God decide that some people could know him and his love, while others were damned to hell? Do we really believe in that? That's what the Bible study literature said." She paused, frowned, and said, "I just want to know what we believe as Christians."

I remember smiling. I had always believed that people whose lives had been changed through an encounter with the living God in Jesus Christ would, sooner or later, begin to ask the significant questions of faith. I thought that the more people read and reflected upon the Bible, the more they would want to know what we as a church believed and why. Now this follower of Jesus, and a number of others since, was asking the questions. Our conversation about the doctrine of predestination and where our church stood led to other questions and other explanations. It was a wonderful conversation on the person and work of Jesus Christ—the one she had met and experienced in worship.

The Bible—and more specifically her experience of its relevance in real time—provided the bridge between the God she had met and her understanding of that God.

The truth of the matter is that doctrinally based ministry has at least two problems. The first is that we often have answers to questions no one is asking, which leads to the second problem: we can get entirely too caught up in theological debates among our churches. Others experience this as the church fighting with itself.

This gets us off the point. When there are so many in our world who have had no experience with Jesus Christ, no invitation to come and see this one to whom the Christian church ultimately points, this wrangling gets in the way. We do not intend it, but it does get in the way. And it's not just about the unchurched. It is also about "de-churching" Jesus for the "overchurched" and absent. And it is about removing the distractions of such infighting for those who have experienced the person of Jesus Christ in our churches and seek more of it as growing disciples.

George Barna was asked by a church to study the unchurched in the Philadelphia area. The church wanted to reach out to those who were not in already established congregations. Members of this church wanted to know why the unchurched were not in church so that they could more effectively minister to these people in partnership with the churches already present. I remember Barna telling us at a pastors' gathering that one of the main reasons people stayed out of the churches was, according to the study, expressed by an old man who said, "Why would I go to church? I've got enough trouble in my life. I don't need theirs. All they ever do is fight among themselves."

Doctrinal debates move this wrangling to the front doors of our churches and make it clear that this is a place only for those who can agree with us or whom we can persuade. Evangelism, outreach, and welcome are, at the least, compromised.

So let's move our theological discussions to the inside of the church. Let's get our focus clear: we are to make disciples (passionate followers) of Jesus Christ. First we need to introduce them—through experiencing the love of God we call grace. Then we can respond to their real-life questions and invite them into theological reflection.

That is when doctrine makes the most sense. That is when doctrine serves the purpose of equipping people for a living relationship with Jesus Christ. Experience is insufficient in itself, but so is doctrine. Together they meet in conversations around our understanding of the revealed Word of God—the Bible.

When these two aspects of our faith—that is, experience and doctrine—are bridged by biblical literacy, then we equip people to move beyond "religion à la carte." Religion à la carte is buffet theology. Religion à la carte is feel-good spiritual consumerism. It is experience with little biblical literacy and even less serious reflection, that is, doctrinal understanding. It has no staying power. The incredible, living relationship with Jesus that discipleship is built on both experience and doctrine as established through biblical learning. Religion à la carte cannot provide spiritual confidence for persons when they need it most. Productive thinking recognizes that both experience and doctrine are brought together through biblical literacy in the life of the disciple Jesus Christ.

Productive thinking can reveal that a false dichotomy between doctrine and experience finds expression most frequently in style. The style of preaching, the style of worship, and the style of presentation have become battlegrounds for resistance to change in our churches. But style is the wrong issue.

I have had the privilege of addressing many assemblies of clergy and laity across the denominational lines. Frequently, the topic is our need to change in order to reach other generations with the gospel. This change is often focused on the "how" of worship. One way I have tried to make such change personal is to begin by asking all of the grandparents to stand up. Then I ask them to sit down only if they would be willing to do anything so that their grandchildren would know Jesus Christ in a personal way. I have yet to have one grandparent remain standing. Then I ask how many parents in the group have a child that is no longer regularly worshiping or attending church in any of its ministries. The number of hands is overwhelming. I ask these parents whether they are willing to keep on doing ministry, keep on worshiping the same way, even though their children are left out of the church.

■□■□■

"I have to tell you what happened on Sunday, Pastor," Thomas, a forty-year-old worshiper said. "I know you sometimes wonder who you are preaching to and whether it is making a difference. Last Sunday I was worshiping with my seventeen-year-old son. After worship, he turned to me and said, 'Now that was a great sermon!' You made a difference in my son's life, and I just wanted to thank you for it."

Any pastor knows that such compliments are testimonies to more than her or his preaching skills. Ultimately, they are a testimony to the presence of the Holy Spirit, without whom such connections simply do not happen. But they are also affirmations of the worship experience itself. The message, the scripture, the illustrations and songs all must work together to have that kind of impact. But isn't that the point of our ministries?

From Observation to Participation to Immersion
(LOOP #2: THE DISCIPLESHIP PATH)

One dichotomy that gets our leaders stuck is that between the form of our worship and the changing forms of cultural expressions. Our world has shifted from observation and reflection to participation. I believe that a productive approach to this polarity leads us to immersion as the creative tension between the two poles.

"Pastor, you've got to do something about the choir." Her voice was insistent. The pastor grimaced inwardly. She knew what was coming. "We need more members. Our choir has dwindled and dwindled. All we have are sopranos, a few altos, and a smattering of men. You need to tell the younger people to get involved, to come and sing with us!"

This scene could come from a thousand churches across our country. The choir lofts of most of our churches show the absence, not the presence, of membership. Our choir members and longtime participants remember the "glory days" of choir, when the loft was full, the voices strong, and the joy of listening clearly evident. But those days are gone. And, apart from a few who remember with longing, most people seem satisfied with that change. Oh, it's not that they wouldn't like to see the loft filled; it's just that it is no longer a high priority for their time or their worship experience.

Choirs and choir lofts were a product of worship as observation. The involvement of the worshiper was assumed in the congregational readings, the hymns, and, when appropriate, in Holy Communion. The rest of the time, worship was assumed to be an end in itself. The leadership of worship was given over to "the professionals," who were not just the clergy, but were the singers and organists as well.

This was a time when meaningful religion was thought to be a cognitive exercise. The person who considered the repetition of worship boring simply didn't understand the inner value of rote worship. This was "modern" worship. Like a machine, it happened the same way, at the same time, like clockwork—consistent, dependable, unsurprising. The power of this worship was that it invited reflection—on the sermon, the words of the anthem, the language of the hymns, and so forth.

But our world has looped. We now have "contemporary worship," praise songs, Taizé mantras, chancel dramas, and video clips in our worship—and people expect to participate in the event, not just observe it. Fewer and fewer people are willing to sit back and observe. Reflection time in worship, without a clearly established purpose and a sense of intention, creates anxiety. Most worshipers assume someone has missed a cue! We have been influenced by the MTV reality: we flow with the images, the sounds, and the words. Only later will we reflect upon them and decide whether or not to integrate them into our lives, our ethic.

The practice of annual meetings, once the hallmark of healthy churches, has collapsed. We still have them, but most pastors and council members dread them because primarily those with an axe to grind show up. We play at being a democracy, but so few come to our annual meetings that we often have to mount a last-ditch phone campaign to get a quorum. This is not democracy. It is an oligarchy: rule by a few. Our people are telling us that they would rather *participate in something significant* than vote on something legislative. All the vital signs of a ministry (worship attendance; involvement of children and parents, of seniors and singles; the financial health and the maintenance of the building and grounds) can be in good order. But the annual meeting continues to flag. The only exception seems to be when a church fight exists, a senior minister is being called, or a major issue with the building and grounds is being discussed.

Participation and Immersion

Worship needs to move in a more visceral, participatory direction as well. With praise songs, Taizé worship, and the use of audiovisual technology, worship becomes an engagement of the body and soul. This has always been a hallmark of African American Protestant worship. Now, just as soul, R&B, and hip-hop have moved into mainstream America, so must soulful worship. From participation, worship moves to immersion. The individual can get lost in the power, the poetry, the beauty, and the transcendence and immanence of the Spirit of God in Jesus Christ. The music and prayers—even the preaching—become participative. Piano beneath the words of the sermon, video clips, or drama organized around the theme of the worship and prayers invites the participants to let the Spirit move them. No wonder the fastest-growing churches are those that have adopted not just participation as a worship goal, but immersion as well.

Once again, however, immersion is not the last stop on this excursion of our time. The spiritual leader will intuit that we are about to loop yet again. Immersion invites reflection and an observation about the holiness of our God and the nearness of God's love.

"We thank you, our God, that you have said that no prayer is too great nor any too small for you to hear and respond in the wisdom of your infinite love for us," I prayed. "So we lift our personal prayers to you, each one of us in the sanctity of our own hearts, in this moment of silence." I waited, counting silently to myself . . . and you could have heard a pin drop in the quiet.

Engaged people are prayerful people. Immersed people are reverent people.

"I can't tell you how much it means to me that you give me time in worship to pray. The first time you did that, I thought, 'Wow, this is cool.' After that, I didn't even stop to think. I just prayed." My friend Pete was talking. We were on our way to fly fish in Yellowstone National Park. Pete is an outdoors type. Dressed in Orvis fishing attire, he was talking about worship and prayer as we drove across Montana—and I hadn't even brought it up!

Participation is the doorway to full encounter: the head, heart, soul, and life. When God's people participate and then become immersed in a holy moment, it informs their reflections and observations about all of life—not just worship.

What's the point? Discipleship is the point. Life transformation is the point. Life change that impacts the daily decisions and interactions we face in the presence of the Savior we know as Jesus Christ is the point. This is an outcome that changes the world in that place and time when the disciple examines the situation through the lens of faith and then acts in that power.

From Self to Relationship to Self-Full Relationships
(LOOP #3: PERSONAL PIETY AND JUSTICE)

Productive thinking will also discover that because it is about spiritual transformation, it must be about justice and compassion. Jesus Christ has a habit of bringing the world with him when he enters a human life. The world he brings is filled with all the diversity and complexity of the life that our creator has given us. When Jesus Christ changes lives, those people are no longer just about themselves. The Savior calls us from self to relationship to self-full relationships.

■□■□■

He was driving home when he saw her: an old woman struggling with two heavy bags of groceries. He went by and felt that inner tug. Turning around, he stopped and asked if he could help.

"Well," she said, "I sure could use a ride to my place. It's not far."

So, after he introduced himself as a doctor and a Christian, she got into the car and he drove her home. As he helped her inside with her groceries, she said, "I sure could use a ride to my church. I haven't been in a while, and I'd like to go to services tonight. I hate to ask you, but my other rides would be there by now."

So he dropped her off at church—and waited there for her. She said, "Thank you. You sure are a fine Christian. Thank you. Thank you."

When he got home, he explained to his wife why he was late. She looked at him and said, "Good for you." And he said that it really was his pleasure.

There is a joy that comes with serving. We believe that our God has created us in God's image. It is the very nature of our God to give, to serve in love. We know this because of the coming of the savior Jesus Christ. It is not surprising that it is, therefore, at the heart of the human spirit to give. This impulse strives against the urge to "take care of number one."

Maturity brings with it the possibility of setting aside one's self and caring about others instead. When the self is triumphant, relationships suffer; other people suffer. The follower of Jesus knows that we are called to reach out in care and concern to our neighbor. The self is called into community—that is, into relationships. The triumphant self asserts itself at the expense not only of people, but of social systems and justice.

Justice is the natural extension of a personal faith. Personal faith is not private faith, which uses religion as an insulation against the world. Private faith is an anesthetic that numbs the conscience to the needs of the poor and to the injustice of our politics and institutions. Yet the prophet Micah, speaking for our life-giving God, writes: "With what shall I come before the Lord, and bow myself before God on high? Shall I come before him with burnt offerings, with calves a year old? Will the Lord be pleased with thousands of rams, with ten thousands of rivers of oil? Shall I give my firstborn for my transgression, the fruit of my body for the sin of my soul? He has told you, O mortal, what is good; and what does the Lord require of you but to do justice, and to love kindness, and to walk humbly with your God?" (Micah 6:6-8).

I have always been struck by the fluid movement between personal and social requirements in this passage. We are called to "do justice," which I understand means to work for the creation of opportunities for all—not just that they might make a living but that each might discover her or his gifts, talents, and capabilities and develop them as fully as possible. This places the person of faith within the arena of social and political systems. But how shall we respond?

Changing the World

The day has long passed when passing a resolution changed the world. Changed lives change the world. Transformed lives, informed by the expectations of God's heart, work to do justice—in our personal lives as well as in the institutions and communities in which we work and play. This is not a matter of passing resolutions. Rather, it is a matter of making a different world. The outcome of our efforts is the point. We dare not feel self-satisfied with the goodness of our motivations. For years, we have believed and worked for the idea that people of all races and creeds should have equal access to opportunity. Yet the gap between us still exists. Perhaps it is time for us to set aside all the conversation and political debate and to "do justice." By that, I mean that the Christian church gets side tracked in controversy, yet the hungry still go unfed, the poor are still in need, the prisoner lacks dignity with accountability, and the disenfranchised remain on the edge of society. God's active love demands more than that.

Evangelism without justice is an empty hope. Justice without the name of the one in whose name we serve is suspect of motive. On the one side is private religion. On the other side is do-goodism. Neither changes the circumstances of those to whom God calls us. If we must continue to debate and pass resolutions, then let them have a requirement for action. And beyond the resolutions, let us look for partners wherever and whenever we can find them who actually change the world to better reflect the love of the God we know in Jesus of Nazareth.

As I have already suggested, this postdenominational world opens the doors to forming innovative partnerships and strategic alliances based upon our shared values. Let us never hesitate to name the name of Jesus and to work with those who share this same conviction. Let us work with those outside our faith when our values and beliefs are respected and the outcomes of our joint efforts move our society and world closer to the ideal of God's kingdom.

The prophet Micah did not stop with "do justice." He articulated, in the voice of the God who alone is God, that we are to "love kindness." From doing justice (an outcome-driven effort), we are called to "love" charity. My friend demonstrated this second expectation from the heart of God. How many people in our time hunger for a simple act of kindness as a sign of hope in their unjust circumstances?

Several years ago, I read a disturbing conjecture by a pastor. He wondered aloud, for how many of those who come to church is the pastor's handshake the only human contact they receive in a week that is economically or sexually neutral? One wonders how many points of conversation that woman had the week before my friend gave her a ride, first to her home and then to her church. Simple kindness is linked by the prophet to justice. One is a social responsibility that strives to change social and political realities. The other is no less a social responsibility—the difference is in the change it works to make. Kindness recognizes on the personal level the dignity and worth of another person.

Evangelism without kindness is spiritual tyranny. The other is neither valued nor affirmed, except as one who has been recruited to my faith point of view.

Self-Full Relationships

Self-full relationships recognize the personal and social aspects of God's love active within the person of faith. Individual worth and social justice are two sides of the same coin.

■□■□■

"Prince of Peace saved my marriage," he said. The young couple with small children had been separated. Their marriage was on the rocks, but they weren't able to pronounce it D.O.A. So they decided to begin to go to church together. After a journey of many months, they visited with another pastor on staff and asked if he would "remarry" them. They were prepared to make a spiritual commitment to each other and to their children this time. This time, they would first "walk humbly with their God."

Relationships of all types are healthy to the degree that the individual is not tyrannized by the relationship but is fully engaged in it. This can happen only when both persons are valued as authentic. This happens best when the eternal love of God undergirds the commitment they share with each other.

The goal is self-full relationships. That is what this young couple discovered in the life of faith. The self cannot be fully alive without the social because we are created for relationships. Social responsibility is the natural expression of self-full relationships. When our personal relationships are whole, we naturally seek to create wholesome social and political relationships.

The Christian is a growing self within our culture who will *necessarily* strive for justice. The reason is simple. As we discover and live our eternal value before the savior Jesus, we are compelled to seek such valuing of all and by all. No wonder the great personal pietists of our time and history have been compelled to seek provision for the poor and disenfranchised. One need only reflect on the lifework of Mother Teresa to see the clear connection between personal faith and social concern. Granted, this is a wonderful and ideal example. However, this compassionate outgrowth of an intimate and living relationship with Jesus Christ is, I would argue, much more the norm than not. In our own history, people on both sides of the abortion or capital punishment debates have more frequently than not shared a strong, personal belief system. They might not agree with one another on all the issues, but their motivation for valuing others is the *personal experience of being valued by the God of Jesus Christ.* And none have been content simply with passing legislation. The legislation they have sought is but the prelude to "doing justice," expressing "loving-kindness," and "walking humbly with our God."

I do not mean to suggest that the passing of appropriate laws is not necessary. Such a position would be, at best, naive. Rather, I believe that the test of such legislation is in its effects on the lives of those it seeks to aid. Tragically, many great laws have languished because they were not sufficiently implemented. Christians know that implementation is the key—and changed lives are the final desired outcome.

Let me be clear. Any man who has experienced the love of God in Jesus Christ and does not insist on equal valuing of women simply fails to grasp the power of the incarnation. Any parent or adult who has known the wonder of being a child of the creator and still abuses children has simply not been confronted with the biblical witness on the sanctity of children before our God. Any spouse who has experienced God's forgiving power in Jesus Christ and still abuses his or her mate lives in contradiction with the essence of God's life-sustaining power available to all in Jesus, who blessed the woman at the well and set her free with his love. Any Christian who cannot or does not see in any other person—regardless of race, ethnic origin, or creed—the face of the Savior simply lives in tragic ignorance of the God she or he has met and come to trust.

New thinking reveals how connecting strands of life continue to weave us and apparent opposite categories together. Personal faith and social justice, individual encounter with the living God in Jesus Christ, and relational healing are like couples dancing together and then apart. They spiral and intersect in life-giving ways. The either/or of yesterday becomes the both/and of today.

Addressing "Hot" Issues

This interweaving is equally evident in the political sphere of our lives. We have moved from seemingly rigid categories of liberal and conservative to centrist and now to synthesized polarities. A remarkable blurring of the lines has occurred. Fiscal conservatives oppose capital punishment. Social liberals oppose greater government involvement in charitable institutions for the sake of their effectiveness. The categories are, quite simply, no longer clear.

■□◪□◩

"The ultimate source of our decision about homosexuality cannot be the social context in which we live," he said. "Rather, as Christians, we must seek God's Word and, when it is silent, look to the living Word, Jesus Christ. And the only pertinent text is Romans 1."

I was intrigued. Here was a Christian leader who was willing to prayerfully take us back to the Bible for conversation about this explosive issue in the church and our culture.

"The truth of the matter is that Romans 1 wasn't originally Romans 1. Let me state the obvious: the original Greek had no chapters and verses. What we now call Romans 1 was a continuous thought with what we now call Romans 2. If we read it this way, then none of us gets out of Romans 1, so called, without sin. The only question is how it gets us to Romans 2: 'Therefore you have no excuse; whoever you are, when you judge others; for in passing judgment on another you condemn yourself, because you, the judge, are doing the very same things.'

"So, I understand the biblical text to call us away from judging and toward the forgiving love of Jesus Christ, which we have already received. And this sets the context within which we talk of these issues. The call to forgiving love includes those with whom we disagree. This ought to especially be the case within the church. Yet we see it is often the opposite case. So let us welcome one another as forgiven sinners. Let us become the church of Christ's welcoming love, not the community of controversy that we have so often become."

What an interesting way to get at it. And how could I characterize or categorize his position? It seemed that he was biblically conservative but socially liberal. Maybe this is the productive thinking that finally can unite our disagreements. The authority of God's word is upheld. The challenge is to understand how we use God's word and in what spirit the Bible is to be used to affirm and set loose the faithful. Biblically conservative and socially liberal weave the strength of the Word into the warmth of Christian compassion and our faithful zeal for justice. I don't know, in this case, whether I agree with all the implications of his reasoning. But I like the model. A model grounded on God's word is a model that calls for respectful conversation.

Finances and Mission

I have never forgotten noted author on Christian social justice Tom Sine telling us, "Don't tell me where your mission heart is. Show me your budget and I'll tell you where your mission heart is."[7]

The church has not always been financially honest. Oh, I don't mean that we intentionally misled anyone, let alone misappropriated funds. Rather, I have seen again and again how our budgets have been used as a smoke screen to cover financial irresponsibility. We move one fund to cover another and only rarely ask whether this process is responsible, let alone ethical. Our ministries will gain great credibility when we can simply show where our monies have gone and what they have accomplished. As we develop more open fiscal processes and policies, our businesspeople will trust us more and will entrust us with more of their resources. Apart from staff salaries (which I believe are private until the entire congregation is willing to reveal their tax statements!), the flow of income and expenses ought to be simple enough that anyone can understand it. And when we cover one ministry with other ministries' funds, let us at least dare to ask the question, Is this a ministry worth continuing when it cannot financially sustain itself?

And Sine is right. Our mission is decoded in our budget. (Actually, our ministries do not have "budgets." We have spending plans that are only loosely based on pledges. *Budget* is too firm a word for the tools we use to manage the funds entrusted to us.) What we spend our funds on *is* our mission. If the mission is working, if lives are changing and the world is being affected by the love of Christ, then let us not apologize for how we use our funds.

The critical question is whether we are willing to be fiscally responsible at the same time that we will be faithfully risking for the sake of the gospel as it intersects culture and changes lives. A failure of nerve, rather than financial prudence, more frequently causes the failure of our ministries to expand and reach out. I have learned from businesspeople that calculated risks are critical to business success. In fact, in our world today, the companies that fail to risk strategically are usually those that fail . . . period.

We have lost the option of risk-free ministries. This means that we will be called, sooner or later, to have our spending plan serve the mission of our churches. Obviously, this isn't an excuse for ignoring the financial realities. Rather, it is the way that we keep the point of transformed lives and a transformed world at the heart of what we do.

So we have entered between opposites once again as we move from the personal to the corporate. Now we finish the sequence by connecting the two in personal service.

Personal Service

"Happy Thanksgiving," I said. My wife and I were hosts for the annual Thanksgiving meal at the Salvation Army in Minneapolis, Minnesota. We had arrived in time to meet the staff and the other volunteers. Since we were willing to meet those who came, we got to be the welcoming arm of the Salvation Army on this occasion.

"We're glad you're here," my wife and I said as we greeted individuals and families.

"Thank you. Thank you."

The reply was most frequently said with genuine gratitude and, when eye contact was made, a sudden smile would erupt on weather-creased faces and careworn eyes would crinkle and light up. Then the response most often heard was, "I'm glad to be here too."

What a privilege it was to shake hands and greet perfect strangers! I had a sense that Jesus Christ would meet us there that Thanksgiving. And he did. Over and over again, we saw the light of Christ in the laughter of children who could eat their fill, in the quiet satisfaction of street people as they dug into turkey, mashed potatoes and gravy, and dressing. Their genuine gratitude for the simple joy of a traditional Thanksgiving meal elevated the level of gratitude in our hearts. All the way home, Chris and I talked of how we had been the ones blessed . . . and prayed that Christ had met at least some of those who came in the warm welcome we and the others there had tried to offer.

Worship is an experience of the love of Jesus Christ. Personal service is one way that the Christian extends that experience into the lives of others. Acts of kindness, deeds of justice, and walking humbly with God—personal service—bring our faith into real life. Each act in its own way tilts this world toward the kingdom of God as we meet it in the savior Jesus. And we, as followers of the Savior, are brought closer to the heart of God and stand firm on the ground of his love. Once a Christian has experienced this extension of faith, he or she cannot, will not, go back to a life without it.

Knowing Our Business and Our Culture

Jim Collins, coauthor of the book *Built to Last*, was addressing a group of senior pastors from across the country. He had shared with us the research that led to the book's publication and some of the critical learnings from it. He said that visionary companies, which had stood the test of time and significant transition, knew what their businesses were. They had a firm grasp of their core beliefs even as they created mechanisms to stimulate progress continually. Then he asked us if we knew what our congregation's unique "business" was. Looking at us with concentration, he said we really couldn't know unless we could answer a simple question. Then he asked simply, "What are you willing to go out of business for?" Usually talkative leaders from many denominational and geographical contexts, we were stunned into silence.[8]

What is the church willing to go out of business for? For what is a denomination, a congregation, or a ministry willing to risk it all? In other words: what's the point?

Gandhi is reported to have said, "We must first become what we seek to create." Can the Christian church become the community of saints and sinners that strives to become the model for transformation in the twenty-first century? I believe we can. I believe God's Holy Spirit will lead us to do so. This will not be cost free. As Dietrich Bonhoeffer reminds us from the Germany of the Nazis, grace is always a costly grace.[9] Are we willing to go out of business for this "costly grace" of God's love in Jesus Christ? The answer will be transformative. First the culture of the church will have to change. Then the culture(s) in which we minister will change.

Edgar H. Schein writes, "What really drives the culture (of any organization)—its essence—is the learned, shared, tacit assumptions on which people base their daily behavior. It results in what is popularly thought of 'the way we do things around here.' . . . Life (within the organization) becomes predictable and meaningful."[10] The results are that any culture is multifaceted and deeply embedded in the how and why of getting things done. Schein further asserts three critical truths about culture: (1) culture is deep, (2) culture is broad, and (3) culture is stable.

But culture is not ignorant—at least not in its formation. The culture of any organization is the composite experience and learning of a group of people that has led to success. The present ideas and behaviors within a culture have been established based upon previous successes.

Doing Things the Same Way

The problem is that the strategies and methods that led to past successes may undermine present and future achievements. To continue to follow these patterns unconsciously is a form of success addiction. We become addicted to past strategies and goals because *at one time they worked.* In the face of fewer achievements, success addiction blinds us to the possibility that the repetition of doing things the same way we always have may ensure failure, not success.

Albert Einstein is reported to have said, "Insanity is doing the same thing over and over again and expecting different results." Jesus taught us the same thing when he said that no one puts new wine in old wineskins or patches an old garment with new cloth. The old wineskins will burst with the fermenting of the new wine. The old cloth will be torn as the new cloth shrinks. But how many of our churches are stuck simply patching the tears in our ministries with the new cloth of a "new program"? How many of us continue to do the same old things in the same old way—yet we expect different results? We need a culture shift in the church.

Edgar Schein identifies why this is so difficult to accomplish. He writes: "Culture matters . . . because the beliefs, values, and behavior of individuals are often understood only in the context of people's cultural identities."[11] No wonder changing how we do things is so difficult. It is not simply a matter of change. The underlying problem is our identity. To make transformational change, we must transform how we think *about ourselves.* To the degree that how we do things is linked to our very identity, we will hang on to them until it becomes clear to us that we are choosing to "go out of business" for them. Are we really willing to go out of business for the forms of what we do? Is a core piece of our identity how we do worship rather than whom we worship?

Change and the Church's Self-Understanding

Recently, in my denomination, we embraced a number of other denominations. This was a strategy to break down the walls between various Protestant groups. Apart from the process that grew directly out of the "old ecumenism," most of these initiatives caused barely a ripple. But when the Lutherans embraced the Episcopalians, a furor erupted. The Episcopal church has as one of its core identities the "historic episcopate." This is the notion that Episcopal bishops, through the centuries, have an unbroken line of succession and authority from the apostles through the physical laying on of hands. If the two communions (Lutheran and Episcopal) were to come together, the historic episcopate was deemed necessary in order for Episcopalians to maintain their identity.

On the other hand, some Lutherans defined as part of their identity the Reformation principle of freedom from such ecclesiastical requirements. The result was a clash, a collision of two cultures. The upheaval within the Evangelical Lutheran Church in America was surprising to some leaders only because they failed to understand the power of culture. The "how" of things was not the issue. The identity linked to that strategy for maintaining the denominational cultures was the issue.

The Episcopal church has decided that it is willing to "go out of business" for the historic episcopate. Some Lutherans assert that they are willing to "go out of business" for a system that will not impose this. Many are left wondering whether this identity clash could have been avoided.

When the "how" gets confused with the "what" of the church, the issue is our self-understanding. In their monumental work *The Churching of America 1776–1990*, Roger Finke and Rodney Stark boldly overturn many of the assumptions by historians of religion in the United States. Their studies, for example, undo the commonly held idea that religious fervor and involvement in the United States are a cyclical phenomenon. What appeared to be a rising and falling cycle was actually the moving of religious fervor from culturally recognized and accepted forms and denominations to newly emerging expressions. Finke and Stark write: "To the degree that denominations rejected traditional doctrines and ceased *to make serious demands on their followers*, they ceased to prosper. The churching of America was accomplished by aggressive churches *committed to vivid otherworldliness.*"[12]

Enculturated religion is adaptive religion. In the name of relevance, I would argue that such religion has forgotten its focus, its core purpose. Without realizing it, as Finke and Stark document, culturally adaptive churches have chosen to die for their adaptations. The core purpose of changed lives and a changed world is hidden under the adaptations.

My personal conclusion from Finke and Starke's work is a spiritual insight. When the church gets so caught up in the culture around it that it reduces its spiritual expectations to the cultural norms themselves, the Holy Spirit moves to those persons and expressions where this confusion is not present. The command of Christ has not changed. Our task as his church is to make disciples—not simply to increase our membership. Discipleship is the liberating paradigm for ministry.

■□■□■

"We want you to know why we are joining this congregation." His eyes were earnest, and his wife nodded. "It's important to us that you know," she added. Then he continued, "We joined this church because of the Marks of Discipleship. This is the first church we have ever participated in where faith is expected to make a difference in how a person lives. Then you and the other staff have taught us how to take church home with us."

"Pastor," his wife said with a smile, "don't ever stop expecting us to be disciples of Jesus Christ. It changes everything."

There was a time when this kind of conversation would have been only a dream. Now, with discipleship as the outcome toward which everything we do is oriented, these conversations happen all the time. And they have energized our ministry.

The Protestant church in the United States has shifted from success to lethargy as it has moved through the 1950s into the 1960s and 1970s and now into the twenty-first century. The remarkable success of the Protestant church since World War II has been clearly documented. Based upon that success, it has developed a variety of cultures that institutionalized the strategies and methods that we identify with this religious boom.

As we moved from the mid-1960s through the 1970s and into the 1980s, many of our churches adapted to the social movements that turned so many institutions on their ears. The Protestant church in the United States survived the social disruption of the 1970s and the greed of the 1980s. We have limped into this new century, and many of our leaders are burned out or discouraged. Most of us now know that a new program will not open this century to the gospel of Jesus Christ.

The Church's Mission

Matthew's Gospel records the mission of the church: "Go therefore and make disciples of all nations, baptizing them in the name of the Father and of the Son and of the Holy Spirit, and teaching them to obey everything that I have commanded you" (Matthew 28:19-20).

The DNA of the church is mission. That mission is defined not by certain forms but by a clear outcome—to make disciples. The strategies are clear: baptize and teach to obey.

This is not a low-expectation ministry. The expectation is high—and its implications are profound. The Savior expects the Christian church to change lives and, by extension, to change the world God loves. This loop, this dance of opposites, is from success to lethargy to mission—which connects us to the only success that matters.

What is the point? Discipleship. What are we willing to go out of business for? Transformed lives with confident faith in Jesus Christ. Why? Because impassioned followers of Jesus Christ will necessarily be led into the world to, according to the prophet Micah, "do justice, and to love kindness, and to walk humbly with [their] God."

2.
De-institutionalize the Institution

■□■□■□■□

At the annual conference of the Peter F. Drucker Foundation for Nonprofit Management on October 30–31, 2000, Dr. Drucker said: "A healthy society requires three vital sectors: a public sector of effective governments; a private sector of effective businesses; and a social sector of effective community organizations, including faith-based organizations." Drucker further stated that the talk of transition triggered by the new economy is "exactly like the preceding one. What is new is society. The next century will be dominated by society, not the economy. We are entering the first century in human history in which, in the developed world, the great majority of people will work with what is between their ears, not their hands."

Drucker noted: "The twentieth century was one of big government and big business. The next century will be focused on the social sector and its performance. Beginning in the U.S. and other nations, success and survival depend on it." Speaking to leaders of the nonprofit world, including churches, Drucker continued: "You, in this room, have the challenge, the responsibility of the social sector. This is the new challenge: *to innovate, perform, to go from good intentions to results.*"[1]

What a challenge to the church! If Drucker is correct, then the new environment in which churches minister will be one largely defined by a thinking and feeling society. This is not a re-creation of the Enlightenment. Thinking will not serve manufacturing. Instead, it will be the other way around. Products will be developed and their marketing and distribution implemented in keeping with the beliefs, values, and ethics (!) of a thinking and feeling society. In other words, institutions, as we have known them, will be turned upside down. This is the nature of experience, as I have already suggested. Our institutions, whether government, business, or nonprofit, will serve the experience of individuals and families.

From Intentions to Results

As dramatic as this may seem, it is even more radical for our churches to be called "from good intentions to results." This is a radical cultural shift for at least two reasons. The first is that we have operated out of "good intentions" for a long time. We have not done so without an expectation of results, however. Rather, we have presumed that our good intentions would create outcomes—we just didn't feel the need to identify those expected or desired outcomes.

That is the second reason this is such a dramatic shift for us in the churches. We have not clearly identified the results, other than in terms of membership growth or increased giving. Even these outcomes of ministry have been called into question. How much, for example, is membership growth a by-product of a growing community? How can a growth in giving be separated from the larger cultural economy? These questions, among others, have pushed leaders in the church to look to the anecdotal or "soft" data of ministry for outcomes.

If, however, the expected outcome of ministry is spiritually changed lives, then the "soft" results can be substantiated by corresponding "hard" data.

Jesus told them another parable: "The kingdom of heaven is like yeast that a woman took and mixed in with three measures of flour until all of it was leavened" (Matthew 13:33). The effectiveness of our ministry will be visible beyond itself. Just as the leaven does not make up the whole of the bread dough, so the spiritual transformations of individuals and families will not make up the entire community in which we live. But we ought, as I have argued previously, to see the results in a more compassionate and just society. The results will include personal and congregational behaviors. Such outcomes are insufficient in themselves, however, as Drucker infers. They must also result in a changed world, a world in which God's valuing of people and creation is not only increasingly visible but also the emerging norm. Given the cultural context that Drucker has described, this is our great opportunity.

Let the church of Jesus Christ become God's leaven of peace and justice through spiritual renewal. Let us transform our good intentions into results generating efforts. We must de-institutionalize the institution and move into effective ministry for the sake of the gospel of Jesus Christ and the world he came to save.

From Credentials to Gifts
to Effectiveness
(LOOP #4: MINISTRY LOOP)

The next loop or spiral of leadership for the Christian church is from credentials to gifts to effectiveness.

David Messner is the CEO of Park Nicollet, a major health care provider in the Upper Midwest. Speaking at "*Next*Church," a conference held at Wooddale Community Church in Eden Prairie, Minnesota on October 14, 2000, he said, "Knowledge is now available to anyone who has the time to pursue it." He went on to tell about physicians whose patients had researched their illnesses and possible treatment plans and had come into the exam room with a wealth of information that historically had been available only to the professional. The outcome of the reality that anyone can research almost anything on the Internet is, according to Messner, that "there is no medical hierarchy."

The professions in the Western world are undergoing immense changes. Credentials used to be the basis for higher value. An M.D. was a "union card" that provided access to learning and information not available to anyone else. With this access came prestige and entitlement. Physicians were held in high esteem within the community and rewarded financially and in terms of position. That is no longer the case. As the financial realities of health care continue to dictate possible treatment plans, as the information once held to a select constituency becomes universally available, and as the expectations for access to the best in treatment by anyone increase, the autonomy, privilege, and entitlement of physicians become a stumbling block to effective health care.

The same can be said for clergy. Pastors were once accorded a certain level of respect because they were among the most educated in the community. That is simply no longer true. Similarly, the days of clergy discounts have passed. We live in a postcredential world.

The Christian church should be equipped for this context. The Bible speaks less of credentials than of gifts. Many church leaders, ordained and nonordained, have encountered others more gifted in the areas once reserved for the pastor. When I ask pastors how many of them have met members of their churches who are more spiritual and better at prayer and care than they are, the number of hands is always the majority. Yet pastors often feel compelled, in the very presence of these gifted people, to give the prayer, the care, and the insight required, which weakens the effectiveness of the church's ministry. Having the credentials does not necessarily mean possessing the gifts.

Just because a pastor has formal theological and pastoral education does not mean that she or he is *effective* in those areas. As long as ordained clergy claim position and authority, and feel entitled to certain benefits by virtue of their credentials, they will labor in a world that has disappeared. The hierarchy of credentials has collapsed. What remains is a wonderful egalitarian culture in which gifts can be identified, called forth, and commissioned.

Church leadership must loop from credentials to gifts to effectiveness. If we are willing to serve as spiritual catalysts, we will open the doors of our ministries to a wide variety of people in this new society who desire purpose and significance. Purpose and significance have to do with my particular gifts and talents being tapped and turned loose to accomplish something I believe in. Such effective ministry simply is not possible as long as the pastor clings to the vestige of power that his or her ordination represents. Beyond credentials, we discover gifts and talents. Where the pastor is "inadequate," others have the opportunity to serve with distinction and significance. Anyone can have the information—the number of Bible study and theological courses available to anyone with the time to pursue them is staggering. Those with gifts and passion have the power to transform that information into effective ministry by applying it to real life. The key is to honestly identify our gifts, passions, and talents. Then we can focus them in ways that empower the faith community to move past good intentions to effectiveness.

Our seminaries, Bible schools, and church-related colleges and universities can and should help people identify their gifts and capabilities. The call to ministry belongs to every person who follows Jesus Christ. The call to pastoral ministry is a call to a practice of leadership that is equipped with particular training for the sake of the whole church. Church leadership is effective when it sees any given credential as one of a constellation of gifts with which God has equipped and staffed the church of the savior Jesus Christ.

Those with credentials must see that they are partners with others in ministry. Just as a physician is a partner with technicians and nurses as well as with the patient, so pastors are called to partner with others who are gifted and passionate for being the spiritual leaven in our world. Hierarchy has collapsed—*except as it serves the health of those whose lives the institution can transform.*

What is the particular gift of the ordained? The pastor brings to the conversation three specific things. First is a larger theological and historical perspective, which can be brought to bear on any particular conversation related to ministry. Second is the relationship that the pastor has with the community of faith and the individuals themselves. Third, the pastor often has formal relationships that can be used to form helpful partnerships or collaborations.

To de-institutionalize the institution is not to fail to organize Christ's church. But the organization of the church serves the outcome of spiritual renewal, in individuals, families, and the world. Institutions are accountable for the outcomes for which they exist. This is no less true of the church than for any other organization or institution in our world. The emerging society will hold us more and more accountable to this standard. And falling back on the privilege of credentials will simply not do.

Ministry Teams

"I have never had so much fun in the ministry," she said. This pastor of an urban congregation was enthusiastic, and her enthusiasm was contagious. "Since we have organized into teams, I don't feel like it all rests upon my shoulders. I have wonderful partners. And we can trust one another. I know that they will keep me informed as needed. They know that they are responsible to get certain things done, and they have the authority to carry out their responsibilities. It took a long time to set up this partnership, but it was worth it. Now we are having fun . . . and we are a lot more productive to boot!"

Ministry effectiveness will be directly related to our willingness and ability to form teams. Teams are not possible in a world infatuated with credentials. Teams also are not effective where individual uniqueness and contribution are discounted. Teams become a powerful and strategic tool for ministry when all recognize that "together we know more than any one of us."

For this pastor to shift to teaming required a commitment to engage others in ministry based on their passions and gifts. Teaming meant that, sooner or later, she would have to "turn them loose." She would eventually need to trust the gifts and calling of her partners in ministry. Working with others for effectiveness in ministry means creating the power of teams. The power of teams is directly related to aligning the members of the team to the objective of their efforts, calling for the conscious using of their gifts, and then trusting the team and the Holy Spirit to get the job done. The accountability of the team is to the community in which they serve, to the team itself, and to the outcomes produced. This is the new world of ministry to which Drucker is calling the Christian church.

How does a leader effectively recruit and form teams?

■□■□■

"Pastor Mike," she said, "we have an idea for communion distribution. We are wondering if you would let us tell you about it."

"Of course," I said, "but it really goes to our director of worship, Handt."

"Well, we'd feel better if you heard it first and then we could go to Handt."

So I listened. It was a great idea. In fact, it was one that I had suggested to Handt nearly a year previously. But it just didn't seem to fit the practice and piety of Prince of Peace, so I had let it drop. Now a ministry team that had been working to help with our communion distribution procedure for many months had come up with the idea. I told them I thought they should share it with Handt. Their enthusiasm and practical under-standing were persuasive. The changes were adopted: new teams were formed from the old, and the ministry was multiplied.

This is the best way to form teams. Teams that emerge naturally as a response to a particular problem or oppor-tunity have a way of self-regulating for effectiveness. When they understand that they are accountable for their effectiveness, they will implement, evaluate, and inno-vate for the sake of the desired outcome. That particular team has given way to new teams and new ways of adapt-ing for the growth in numbers and the time constraints of our ministry.

Such teams will often self-lead as well. That leadership emerged over time. The leadership wasn't a particular individual but instead was a couple of recognized lead-ers. The solutions to the communion distribution prob-lem and others emerged as members of the team applied their unique perspectives and experiences to enhance the effectiveness and efficiency of our sharing the Lord's Supper.

When teams emerge in response to an opportunity or problem, they can just as easily disband when the issue has been addressed. The team described above simply shifted in membership and focus as we continued to share communion, and other teams—mission teams, for example—have emerged.

Operation Christmas Child is a wonderful ministry to children in poor areas of the world. The concept is simple: At Christmas, fill a shoe box with toys and appropriate items for children. Then distribute these Christmas gifts to unexpecting children. The result has been nothing short of miraculous. Children have experienced Christmas joy in places and ways that they never thought possible.

One of our pastoral team members became convinced that this was a great opportunity for our church, and he set an outrageous goal of ten thousand shoe boxes. The result was an explosion of teams as we shared the goal, the purpose, and invited people to participate. Some of these teams were as unregulated as friends on a purposeful shopping trip or families who shopped together and packaged the shoe boxes. Other participants were recruited and deployed for the collection and examination of each shoe box. From some of those teams emerged leaders for our mission ministry.

Such recruitment is a second way that teams can be formed. The leader seeks out a person (or group of persons) who has demonstrated the passion and talent necessary for meeting a need. The process includes determining who the leader is and what the goal(s) and time frame(s) are. Leaders can recruit their own team, or a team can be created for them. The team's responsibility is to accomplish that for which they have agreed to come together. Continued support and encouragement—usually through the leader—are important and are demonstrated by equipping the teams for success. Leaders will most often identify what they need and when they need it. The ministry, then, serves by responding in appropriate ways. After the team completes a task, an evaluation occurs in order to learn from the project as well as to identify others whose passions and leadership have surfaced. Sometimes a team will be very successful only to discover that there is something more important for them to do. At other times, a team can be quite successful but decide that the time, energy, and costs exceeded the benefits of the ministry. No matter what the outcome, leaders can learn a great deal as they mine the intelligence of teams and look to identify others who can lead.

In all of this, alignment is an essential ingredient that can create momentum. Momentum occurs when there is enough commitment and energy given to an opportunity that it begins to generate its own response. Our experience with Operation Christmas Child was that it created its own surge toward the goal of ten thousand shoe boxes. People totally off the screen of those leading the project identified with the project, acted on the need, and produced wonderful shoe boxes filled with love. That is momentum!

Alignment is not a lockstep process. Rather, alignment allows for much personal discretion as long as the general direction is toward the identified goal. So, for Operation Christmas Child, people shopped in dollar stores as well as upscale department stores. They included items for school as well as toys. Some families worked on their own boxes while others held "shoe box parties" and a number of families packed the shoe boxes together.

Alignment has certain requirements. First is a compelling need. Second is a clear goal. Third is explicit instructions on how to complete the project—for example, what is acceptable in the shoe boxes as well as what is not. Fourth, alignment requires a published deadline. When these requirements come together, teams become very effective, with no one carrying the burden alone. This is truly when ministry becomes "a lot of fun."

Is Faithful Enough?

"God doesn't call me to be successful; God only calls me to be faithful." The pastor was responding to a conversation I was invited to have with a group of ministry leaders in the Upper Midwest. It is a response I have heard a lot. Usually what I hear is, "Don't expect me to make any real changes in my ministry. What I am doing is my understanding of 'doing church.'" And there is truth to what the pastor said.

The problem is that this is only one side of the coin of ministry. Jesus spends as much or more time talking about being *fruitful* as he does about being *faithful*. Neither faithfulness nor fruitfulness is mutually exclusive of the other. In fact, one has to wonder how faithfulness could be other than fruitful!

"Are grapes gathered from thorns, or figs from thistles? In the same way every good tree bears good fruit, but the bad tree bears bad fruit. A good tree cannot bear bad fruit, nor can a bad tree bear good fruit. Every tree that does not bear good fruit is cut down and thrown into the fire. Thus you will know them by their fruits" (Matthew 7:16-20).

Jesus commands us to be fruitful. Faithfulness is not enough. In fact, our Lord suggests that there are only two options: to bear good fruit or to bear bad fruit. Our ministries will be judged by their productivity. Lack of productivity is not an option spiritually.

Bearing fruit in a time of mixed expectations is difficult indeed. There was a time when the fruits of good pastoral ministry were measured in the number of house calls or hospital visits made. These visits translated into lives touched, and the care of the gospel intersected with the real needs of people. However, this is not enough in our time. That is not to say that caring for the sick and shut-in is no longer valuable; rather, such a ministry will not be judged as sufficient as it once was.

To the chaplaincy role of the clergy has been added an expectation of leadership. Simply caring for the needs of our church members is not enough to keep them satisfied and happy.

■□■□■

"It seems like nothing I do is good enough," he said. Serving in a two-point congregation in rural South Dakota, this pastor struggled with his own vision of pastoral care and the rising expectations of his constituency. "It's not like people even know what they want," he continued. "I've asked them. I've asked the church council and the women's ministry. They just think that something is missing. It is so frustrating that, frankly, I am thinking of leaving and trying my hand at public school teaching. I always loved coaching, and I know schools are looking for teachers who are willing to coach. I love the church. . . . I just can't seem to do this ministry thing."

When no one knows how much or what is enough, no one wins. I am not certain what the issues are for this Christian leader. I do know that neither he nor his congregation knows what is lacking. With such a lack of clarity, there is no way he can be fruitful.

I suggested to him that the missing ingredient might be leadership. When he asked me what I meant, I told him that congregations are hungry for a rebirth of mission. "What was the last real mission outreach that your congregation undertook?" I asked.

"I can't think of a thing . . . and I've been here for over five years," he said.

"Can you think of a real mission project or effort for your church?" I asked. "If you can, and you can give yourself to it, you might be able to invigorate your congregation."

Leaders lead. Those elected, by call or ballot, are expected to lead. When that leading is ill defined, those who follow become restless. When the church is turned inward and focused on survival, its members and leaders unconsciously know something is wrong. They may not be able to articulate it, but there is, nonetheless, a sense of disquiet. That frustration is almost always projected onto the visible leader. In our ministries, that leader is usually the pastor.

Contextual Leadership

Effective leadership is always contextual. The mission impulse within God's people is always a historic and spatial reality. This means that it must fit the visible needs of a particular place and time. For that frustrated pastor, this task was to identify that impulse, direct it, and turn it loose. This is not a solitary task but, instead, is another opportunity for teaming. A team of committed and concerned persons can be brought together to assess the needs not of the congregation but of the larger community. Then they can identify one of the needs as a top priority to which their passion and gifts can be directed to effect change. Leadership is the role that calls such reflection and action into being. The spiral or loop is from pastor to chaplain to leader. And, recognized or not, the loop has already been completed in the minds and hearts of those who look to our churches for significance, depth, and transformation.

We are held accountable for bearing fruit. This is not only the expectation of the one whom we follow and serve but also, as Drucker has told us, an assumption of those who populate or visit our churches. Given our current scarcity of time, people within and outside of the church are asking of our ministries, "What difference will it make if I am a part of this? How will it change the lives of others for the good?" Leadership in our ministries provides answers to these questions through clearly identified missions and outcomes.

Every year at Prince of Peace, we have more volunteers than we can use for our Habitat for Humanity projects. For a long while, we have built two or more homes each year with this great organization. The popularity of this mission project supports the expectations of those who seek to give their time and energy for others. Our Habitat projects always have a clear set of expectations and a precise time frame. And the goal of equipping a family with a home through their efforts, and with financial responsibility by partnering with them, strikes a chord in people across many generations.

Can we in the ministry of the church be that clear about what we are doing and what we expect the result to be? The world is longing for such a spiritual institution.

Moving beyond credentials means that we see authority in a different light. Authority is transformed into accountability. Accountability is answered when we can say that we have done what we hoped to do.

When I met with Wally, Denise, and their two beautiful daughters, I was struck by the enthusiasm with which they shared their faith. They had come to a time in their lives when reading the Bible, worshiping regularly, and sharing their lives and wealth had become routine. Wally told me that it had not always been like that. The ministry of Prince of Peace had changed their lives as a couple and as a family. He joyfully told of his buying Bibles for his siblings and of making significant donations to charities that touched his or Denise's heart. Even his business relationships had changed for the better. It wasn't that there were no difficulties. It was, rather, that he knew that every day was touched by the presence of Jesus Christ. The outcome of his faith was a growing honesty and intimacy with those whom he loved and those with whom he shared his business and community life.

When I left their home, I could only thank God for the blessing I had received. I had gone to get to know Wally, Denise, and their children and to share my hopes and dreams of faith. I left with the humble gratitude of one who has seen lives in the grip of God's grace.

Spiritual Accountability

The authority of the pastoral office cannot accomplish the miracle of changed lives and families. Authority has to do with position, and the authority of the pastoral office, with which I do not disagree, is an institutional one. Such authority is necessary for good order.

But nearly every pastor I have had the privilege of speaking with would be willing to set aside such authority for the sake of spiritual accountability. Accountability is about a shared responsibility for a clearly identifiable outcome. Spiritual accountability occurs when individuals, couples, and families accept that they are partners with the Christian church in living and sharing the faith. No one I know believes that church is good for business in any direct way anymore. No one in our society really pays much attention to that. Rather, church is good for changing lives. Pastors can preach and spiritually gifted leaders can lead, but life is a spiritual journey for which the individual, couple, and family are finally responsible. Christian accountability for the leaders of our ministries comes when we recognize our responsibilities both to share God's word and the sacraments and to translate these into real life through the moral and spiritual practices of faith. Christian accountability for followers of Jesus occurs when they accept their responsibility to put such truth and practice into the decisions and behaviors, the values and dreams of each day.

The identifiable outcome is a faith that makes a concrete difference in the lives of those who trust in Jesus Christ. This is not a private religion. Rather, it is an intensely personal relationship with God in Jesus Christ that confronts social, political, and economic issues as well as family and personal ones.

What might happen if the Christian church held itself accountable to be the holy catalyst for the kind of transformation that I saw in Wally, Denise, and their family? What if we constantly asked how we might be more effective in empowering such spiritually directed lives? Perhaps our pastoral care would be more effective, our prayers more connected to real life, and our worship more transferable into the homes and marketplaces of our world.

Roles and Value

When we move beyond credentials, we must recognize the difference between roles and value. A *role* is a position or function. *Value* is the estimation of worth. Each of us will move in and out of many roles in a lifetime. No one gains or loses value before the God we meet in Jesus Christ. God has declared, in the words of the author of Hebrews, *once and for all* our eternal value in the giving of the Son (Hebrews 7:27).

■□◧□■

When Fran came into my office, I had been told that she wanted to speak to me about joining the church. We chatted briefly, and I shared a prayer. Then, since I felt pressed to get on to the next meeting, I began to talk to her about the congregation and our ministry. After sharing a number of the highlights of our church, I asked if she was ready to join.

"Oh, Pastor," she said, and her eyes welled up with tears. "I didn't come to see if your church was good enough for me. I came to see if I was good enough for you and this church."

I was stunned into silence. And I listened as she shared her story. She had been raised in a fundamentalist sect in the southern United States. At age eighteen, she fled her father and family and went to nursing school. While in school she met, fell in love with, and then married a man who became a pastor. Her husband took up with the abuse that she had left behind in fleeing her father. After years of struggle and a number of children, she left her pastor husband and divorced him. Later she married her second husband. He became an alcoholic, and she was now in the process of divorcing him.

She had heard of our church through a friend at work. This fellow nurse had invited her to worship, assuring her that ours was a congregation where she would feel the love of Jesus Christ. She had come and worshiped for a number of months. Now, sitting in my office, tears streaming down her face, she asked, "So, Pastor Mike, now that you know my story, do you still want me in your church?"

"A Samaritan woman came to draw water, and Jesus said to her, 'Give me a drink.' . . . The Samaritan woman said to him, 'How is it that you, a Jew, ask a drink of me, a woman of Samaria?'" (John 4:7-9).

My role was to be pastor. That opened the door for me to express the eternal value that God had already determined for this broken woman—a value announced to the woman at the well in the text above, a value lived irreversibly in the crucifixion of Jesus of Nazareth.

My role as pastor was what led Fran to make that fateful visit to my office. But the role of her colleague and friend was that of a caring witness. The value of this friend's role was beyond any formal role within the church.

The tragedy of our time—both within the church and in our society at large—is that we have confused role and value. We assume that because I am a senior pastor of a large Protestant church, I have more value to the ministry than those with different roles. Nothing could be further from the truth! The truth is that role is equal to function. Value is equal to personhood. God's valuing of persons is without deference to position. In fact, I would assert that frequently role gets in the way of God's spiritual value system.

The rabbis have taught that the heart of a community is revealed in how that community cares for its widows and orphans. I believe that the heart of a congregation is often revealed in how it treats its custodians and support staff. When role becomes an excuse to make unreasonable demands or to devalue another, it is clearly contrary to the gospel. Those of us within the church know that. What we need to understand is that those outside the congregation know it as well and that they are watching, not so much to catch us behaving badly but to prove their deepest hopes that the world could be different.

Fran was my opportunity to live the accepting love of our Savior. Did her life change because of her involvement in our church? Absolutely. In fact, God has given her a marvelous gift of music, which she now uses to write songs of faith.

If we move into accountability based upon clearly identifiable outcomes and the distinction between role and value, then we shift away from control as well. I have no need to control what religious books or CDs Wally and Denise are reading or listening to—as if I could! Neither do I have any need to control Fran and her involvement in the church.

My role as a pastor and leader is, however, to hold them accountable to spiritual growth and involvement in the church in ways that help the congregation achieve its mission and vision. I also have the spiritual responsibility to equip members of the congregation with the tools and practices that empower such growth and involvement.

I remember the first time I heard a song of praise that Fran had written. We were in worship, and during communion I heard a new song. I listened as I served the sacrament. Later I learned that our director of worship had helped Fran put the words and music together, rehearsed the vocalists, and selected the appropriate worship context. And it worked!

Leaders who move into teaming and accountability will have to get used to surprises. No one asked me to approve the words or music. No one asked me if it was all right for this worship or that. I had a team in place who handled it well. I was delightfully surprised.

Learning through Failure

I am not always so delightfully surprised. There have been times when things did not work out so well. I recall how a friend and fine actor entirely forgot his lines in worship. He had not had enough time for rehearsal. The consequence was that the entire service ground to a halt as he stumbled, apologized, and then read from the script.

Was it worth it? Is the possibility of trusting our partners in the ministry worth the risk of the not so delightful surprise? Absolutely. Ninety-nine times out of a hundred, the surprise will be both positive and energizing. And when it isn't? We have a marvelous opportunity both to learn and to live out our forgiving faith in real life.

There can be no real learning without failure. Failure is simply the word we use to identify that moment when we have the most to learn—and are most likely to learn it! Unfortunately, fear of failure dogs the ministry. We fear failure for the embarrassment of the individuals, the ministry, and ourselves as leaders. This inordinate fear of failure keeps us from that mission impulse of which I wrote earlier. It also enslaves us to those sacred seven words: "We've never done it that way before."

Churches need to become what Peter Senge calls "learning organizations." Learning organizations have discovered the power of failure. Learning organizations strive to minimize the humiliation of failure and maximize its learning.[2] Over and over again, I have told the staff at Prince of Peace: "I don't want any flimsy failures. Give me grand and glorious failures, because those are the ones from which we will learn the most. Those are the ones that show that we have been willing to risk for the sake of a goal big enough that it was worth the risking."

What would have happened in the early church if the early missionaries went only to parts of the world where the possibility of failure was negligible? How many missionary journeys would Paul have taken? My suspicion is that Christianity would be a small Palestinian sect today if the Holy Spirit hadn't prodded those early followers of Jesus Christ outside of their comfort zones and into arenas where failure was a grand possibility.

From Institution to Organism to Organizing Organism
(LOOP #5: THE TRADITION-MISSION LOOP)

This leads us to yet another spiral in the de-institutionalizing of the institutional church: from institution to organism to organizing organism.

A creative chaos erupts when an institution moves into the mitosis of an organism. When an organism grows, its cells split again and again (mitosis). Each cell has a part of the previous cell and also has a purpose that moves it to grow on its own—and the splitting continues.

When ministry grows, it often resembles mitosis. Tasks and opportunities are seized by whomever is closest. The church council often has a very difficult time keeping up with all the activity. The staff, no matter how large or small, simply cannot manage it all. From this explosive stage, the formal organizing of the institution must be adapted. Whether it is the four hundred or eight hundred barrier in church growth, the issue is the same: can the institution adapt its formal organization to the free self-replication of this new organism?

Moving from control to accountability shifts our focus from the institution to organizing the organic growth of the ministry. This creates a dynamic tug between the tradition within the "gene pool" of that ministry and the emerging possibilities for mission in its new context. Organizing the organism is a way of saying that leaders must not succumb to the simplistic. The simple answer is to choose between the tradition of the institution and the mission possibilities of the emerging context. The fruitful alternative is to see how both can work together. The faithful choice brings the best of the past into the unknown of responding to new challenges and issues.

■□■□■

Our preschool director was very concerned. Would the change close our school to the community? "If we make our faith clear, very few members of the community will bring their children to our preschool. We have built our school on Christian values that are expressed in our respect for all people and religious traditions. This hospi-tality will be lost if we become more clearly identified with the Christian faith," she said.

This was a difficult struggle. We knew what we were about at Prince of Peace: a clear witness to the gospel that was expressed in a disciple-making ministry. Jesus was "out of the closet" in all of the related ministries of our congregation. Now we were expecting our preschool to align itself to this clearly identified mission. And the resistance was between its institutionalized tradition and the emerging social context of our time and place.

"I disagree," I responded. "I believe that when we know what we truly believe and can appropriately make that known, we can become even more hospitable and respectful of others. In fact, I'll bet most of those whose children are here assume a faith-witness in our practice. All I am suggesting is that we be clear about whom we serve and why we are here. We are not a public school. Nor are we a social service agency. We are a ministry that wants to demonstrate Christ's compassion in how we deal with everyone."

We lost two-thirds of our staff at the preschool. But one year later, our Child Development and Learning Center is full, we tell the Christ story, and we respectfully include Jewish and Islamic holidays in our calendar. Jesus Christ, we believe, would have been as clear and respectful.

We also have integrated our preschool staff into the benefits program of our ministry. To the best of our abilities, the personnel policies and practices are administered equally. We continue to organize this organism of our various ministries so that the best of the past can be brought into our new context and the new problems and opportunities it brings.

The same can be said for our denominations. Denominations must sift through their traditions to bring forth the best of the past so that the present will be positioned to meet the future, not be a slave to the past. How can this be done? The answer is through leadership that constantly lives in the dynamic middle by refusing to make unnecessary, simplistic choices. The institution is no longer the point. The institution must articulate and serve the point of changed lives that change the world in the spirit and name of Jesus Christ.

Living, creating, and growing entities find ways to adapt without losing their identity. Let the church assert its identity as that spiritually grounded and empowered vehicle through which Christ will transform the world that God loves, in mercy and justice. Then let us anticipate failure and conflict as testimonies that we are doing what we are called to do—not as warnings that we have strayed.

As we learn through failure, let us affirm innovation. Innovators are the nuclei of healthy cells, which keep the organism growing. As change agents, they challenge the tradition. In so doing, they help us identify what really matters from that tradition and they open us to new opportunities and methods for our emerging context. When innovators move beyond the identified mission and vision of the church, they are held accountable for the fruit they bear. Identity is established in the tension between who we were and who we are being called to be. Innovators identify the points of tension for us. How and where they grow the church are the grounds for creative dialogue. This dialogue will lead to greater clarity as well as productive change. In the dialogue, we will discover more clearly ourselves—and the mission to which our Savior calls us.

3.
Moving from
Point A to Point B

We were Christmas caroling. My family had a tradition of hosting a caroling party and inviting family friends. In the twilight, we would walk the streets of our neighborhood. We especially targeted those homes where we had a relationship with our neighbors, but we would carol as we moved between houses as well.

I noticed something interesting while caroling. As we walked between the streetlamps that December evening, the singing would wane. Then, as we approached another streetlight or a porch light, the caroling would increase in volume.

At the next transition, I moved to the back of the party. We were singing the old favorites: "Silent Night," "Away in a Manger," "Hark the Herald Angels Sing," and other well-known Christmas carols. The carolers were families from our church—the children had been raised in the church. Most of them had been confirmed in our congregation. Yet, when we moved into the dark and the song sheets we had provided were no longer helpful, these young people stopped singing.

Suddenly it dawned on me that we were in a different time, a different world, than I had suspected. These "churched" young people didn't know even the first verses of some of the best-known and beloved Christmas carols! Later, in conversation with them, I discovered that my conclusion was indeed accurate. The only time these carols were sung was in church. They could no longer be sung or performed in public school. The children heard them on the radio and occasionally over the speakers in department stores, but they had no memory of the words of even the first verses of most of these carols. The exceptions seemed to be limited to the first verses of "Silent Night" and "Away in a Manger."

The world has changed. We all know that. But what is surprising is the depth of that change. Most Christian leaders give only lip service to the profound alterations of the society in which we live. Until that caroling party, I know that I did.

Cultural Memory

I was shocked by the absence of cultural memory demonstrated by the young people who couldn't sing the first verses of those carols. These were religious songs, to be sure. But they were also cultural icons for me and those who grew up in America in my time and before. These icons had slipped from the screen of American consciousness. They are not there today. We can argue about whether this is good or bad, appropriate or tragic, but the fact remains that our world not only has shifted but, in its religious consciousness, has changed altogether.

Religious language—biblical metaphor—is nonsense in today's world. By that I do not mean to say it is ridiculous. Instead, it has no sense. The Judeo-Christian vocabulary, which has been such a significant part of our history, cultural documents, and social consciousness, is lost to many, if not all, of those born after 1970.

Once, we had a consulting group help us learn about ourselves and how we might capture a vision for the ministry of Prince of Peace. Doug Anderson, president of Nehemiah Ministries, addressed our planning team: "The problem with most churches is not that they cannot get a clear picture of where they want to go. Our experience, in almost every case, is that they do not have a clear picture of what is real. Point B, the goal or objective, is clear. But they misdiagnose point A. Most church leaders start too far down the road. The consequence is that they fail. They fail because they presume those to whom they will speak are more knowledgeable, more religious, and more committed than they are."

American Mission Field

Our current context is simply this: North America is quickly becoming a vast mission field. As in most mission fields, we must learn a new language, adopt new practices, and infuse our most treasured symbols with new meaning. To continue to do ministry as if the old world were still here or would return is to misdiagnose point A. Frankly, because of this, it will not matter what point B is determined to be. We will fail in any event.

For some of us, this has led to a bunker mentality. We find a hiding place in the old ways of doing things. Then we infuse those "old ways" with the sacred content of our creeds. When practices become creeds, the church has turned inward. When tradition becomes dogma, we have turned from the present to the past for the sake of comfort and consolation. And the world will not wait.

The tragedy is that we know better. We don't like ourselves after a while. The reason is simple: Christianity is fundamentally a missionary movement. We know that we do not exist for ourselves. When our ministries function as if we do, they become bland and dissatisfying. This unconscious anxiety becomes frustration, which is often projected onto the leader.

Ownership versus Servanthood

John had moved. He was no longer in his congregation's ministry area. He and his wife had always wanted to live on water, so when the property became available and the price was right, they bought their dream. John's phone number had not changed. His commute was longer, but most of his congregation members commuted at least that long. His pager was almost always on, and he spent longer hours at the church.

But it didn't work. People were angry. They felt betrayed and abandoned. They began to meet together and talk about John's lack of leadership and lack of availability. After all, they reasoned, they were paying his salary. They deserved better.

When practice becomes creed, ministry is about control. Membership has become ownership, not servanthood. The issue with John was not his move. It was a bunker mentality that changed ministry to an equation of who owns whom. Who controls whom is the only game in town when the present is threatening and the future fearsome.

Those outside the church see a congregation as a club. For many of our churches, this has been the fundamental change in perception of those within as well as outside of the congregation. So worshipers come to a new church and are treated as visitors. They "shop" for experiences with which they connect in a deep way. Instead of joining, they then test to see whether that experience is authentic.

But consumer spirituality is not just an external phenomenon in our congregations. Our members who like the club the way it has always been also approach ministry as consumers. When the church changes, we react in much the same way as when we become upset and angry if our favorite market changes the arrangement of the grocery aisles.

The Church and Technology

Even in an age when computers have helped us map the genetic code of the human being, when a space station thousands of miles above the earth is repaired by computer signals sent from below, when public schools invest millions in computers so that their students will not fall too far behind others, and when the computer revolution has transformed our offices and homes, countless churches still do not have e-mail. When computer-imaging artists are standard fare in the movies we watch, our worship is still a desert when it comes to incorporating the true icons of our time.

I am not suggesting a haphazard adoption of technology, especially in our worship. I am challenging the notion that visuals, sound, and lights have no place in our ministries. Technology can and must be carefully and reverently used *for the sake of our worship experience.*

Let the church plug in for the sake of our plugged-in world. But let us plug in so that those who are so disconnected may be reconnected to God as well as to one another. How many loners, plugged in to computers in countless ways, will have to "go postal" before we seriously address the discrepancy between the computer world and real life? Keyboard touch cannot replace human touch. The church that is not afraid of but uses technology comfortably will be able to make this message clear. Otherwise, it will have the ring of anti-change, of religion fixated on the past.

The spiral of life moves again: from data to perception to perceptual data.

The truth is that the use of computers for data and its analysis has become a historical footnote. For many in our world, the computer has become perception. The computer is reality in the sense that it defines or, at the least, confirms reality. The world has shifted. Technology has become the servant of perceptual data, which makes sense of our world for us. And in this exercise of technology, spiritual conclusions are shaped. The computer and the technological leaps it has created have become the assumed lenses for spirit in our time.

David Messner, of Park Nicollet Health Care, claims that this has already happened in the medical field. Microbiology has been joined to technology in such a way that the computer now can and will generate treatment outcomes. Physicians can weigh treatment alternatives based on the likely reality they will create.[1] The data produced by this technology not only describes possibilities but shapes our expectations of the future. And the future has a way of fitting our expectations. Data creates perceptions, which shape reality.

The question is whether the church can see the finger of God in this. Where is God active in this shift? When is God's will compromised by this significant reality change? Let the Christian church take seriously this new world and engage it through the gospel. Technology is not the Messiah—Jesus of Nazareth is. But neither is technology the Antichrist.

At our Christmas Eve services, the Bethlehem star that hung above our nearly life-sized Nativity set was technologically superimposed on the cross that hangs in the center of our worship space. Then, when the sermon made the connection between the Bethlehem babe and the crucified and risen Savior, the star faded into the cross. The visual served the verbal. They both were servants of the gospel, and this expression of the Christmas story took seriously that our time sentimentalizes Christmas by separating it from the larger Christian message of salvation. The connection of Christmas to Easter was also the declaration of God come in the flesh. The star and the cross, ancient symbols of our faith, were given additional meaning visually as well as in the words of the sermon.

Point A for us is a technologically sophisticated and comfortable world in which biblical literacy is negligible. There is, nonetheless, a spiritual hunger for God and the symbols that can connect individuals and families to the transcendent. And there is a hunger for connection beyond the computer cable. We are connected to the world through the Internet but disconnected from those with whom we live. Worship and ministry can be a place where point A can establish common ground for moving to point B.

What is point B? A Christian church in effective mission is the only adequate goal for our time and world.

The state of the church is also a part of our point A. When we look at the Christian church in the United States, there is both reason for concern as well as reason for hope.

The Church's Aging Constituency

There is a crisis of constituency in our churches. The boomers, who seemed to be returning to our congregations, did not stay. Their children are not present. In the Evangelical Lutheran Church in America, for example, more than 120,000 children from kindergarten to sixth grade have been lost to the church over the past decade. This reflects much of what has happened across the denominations in our time. This means that we have most likely also lost their parents and older siblings. As if that were not bad enough, it is likely that they will not become adults who identify with the church, let alone worship. Their children will be lost as well, unless we become a missionary church that can meaningfully communicate the gospel in these people's language.

Who is coming? The aging of the Protestant church is obvious. Most mainline denominations admit to an average age that nears or exceeds sixty. Attend most worship events in the United States, and you will see a sea of gray.

The children, grandchildren, and great-grandchildren of these "grays" are not coming to church. A member of Prince of Peace best expressed the reasons for this. He is the son of a pastor. He and his wife were married in a Protestant church, but that was the last time they attended worship for nearly fifteen years. When they joined our church, I asked him why he hadn't come to church in the interim. His response: "We just couldn't see how it would *add any value* to our lives."

We need to be clear. The percentage of adults and teens who worship has not changed in nearly sixty years. The problem is that they come but do not stay. They identify but do not participate. They observe but do not serve. And more and more of those who do come and worship are going to larger and larger congregations. Why? Because those churches are often willing to innovate, make mistakes, and strive to learn for the sake of excellence in presenting the gospel. In short, these churches have not adopted the bunker mentality that afflicts so many of our congregations and leaders.

Leadership Crisis

The leadership crisis in our churches has recently been assessed by Alan Klass. In a study published in May 2000, Klass found that 20 percent of clergy in the Lutheran Church—Missouri Synod (LCMS) were in the advanced stages of burnout, 20 percent were well on the way to that state, 30 percent of the ministers were ambivalent about their work, and only 30 percent of the ministers truly loved their work. Klass's study also included projections of the number of pastors in that denomination. In 1987, over 6,600 pastors were serving in the LCMS. If conditions remain the same, that number will decline to about 2,000 by the year 2017.[2]

In a discussion with Alan, I learned that he had been in conversation with other denominational executives and had concluded that these figures hold true across nine other denominations.

■□□□■

"I am having the time of my life," the pastor said. "Oh, I don't mean to tell you that there isn't stress. There is! It's just that I have decided that we need to try new things in order to reach out. And my leaders are willing to let me do it. They see their kids enthusiastic about church, and they are willing to forgive some of the mistakes I have made. The average age of this church has dropped markedly, so I think it's working. And I love it!"

There are signs of hope out there as well, and they are rarely found in congregations where the old ways have simply been preserved. Promising signs usually emerge in contexts in which leaders have decided to try new things along with some of the old. That is what the pastor did. I didn't learn why he or his leaders made that shift in thinking, but they had clearly moved away from a bunker mentality and into a mission mind-set.

Toward Changeless Changing

The emergence of our ministry horizon means shrugging off the mantle of the sanctified past as the only way of doing our work. The spiral of life continues when we see the significant movement in our time from changeless to changing to changeless changing.

There was a time when the worship and ministry of the church was perceived as changeless. In fact, that was part of its appeal. With the world shifting and, at times, threatening, it was a gift to go someplace where change was occurring on a very limited basis. This seemed to reinforce that we were connecting with the changeless God of Scripture.

One of the sayings that I remember reading and hearing in sermons as a boy was "Jesus Christ: the same yesterday, today and forever." This saying provided a sense of stability, of being grounded in spiritual permanence. This stuff of worship was solid, it seemed to say. There was a continuity between the saints of old and the gathered people of today. That conviction shaped my spirituality. It connected me to my parents and grandparents. Church was worth the investment of my time and life because it had always been worth such an investment.

But then we slammed into the violent 1960s. The church of permanence seemed woefully out of touch with the real world. *Relevance* became the watchword. We had shifted from changeless to changing in our approach to ministry. The crucible of time and social upheaval pushed the Christian church first into resistance and then into adaptation to rapid change. Guitars became the sign of "with-it" worship. Any change seemed worth making. Perhaps the best example of this season of change for change's sake was an ecumenical worship in Chicago in which the Eucharist was offered with the invitation to "dip it, sip it, or skip it." Few observers at the time would have thought negatively about that flippant invitation.

Four years ago, as we were looking at remodeling our worship space at Prince of Peace, I read a series of articles about growing churches in the Twin Cities area. At the very time that we were growing, with an increasing number of young adults in worship, so was the Roman Catholic Cathedral in St. Paul and the Basilica of Minneapolis. Further reading and some conversation led me to conclude that we had turned again in the spiral of life. The highly symbolic surroundings of those churches were a spiritual draw for two generations. There were changes in the worship format and practice—contemporary music as well as organ, paperback worship books as well as new and old hymnody. But the changes were vehicles of that which was perceived as changeless. We had shifted into a season of changeless change.

Changeless change: a season of bringing the best from the past into the real world of today. This is the distinction that Dr. Leonard Sweet of Drew Theological Seminary makes between the container and the content. The content is Jesus and the historic faith of the Christian church with its sacraments and symbols. But the container is variable. The language is of the time, and the songs a blend of those oldies that stir our hearts and the new ones that force a tapping of the toes or the raising of hands in worship.[3]

Lyle Schaller has said that churches historically have changed once every forty years.[4] Now we must change at least every decade. But what we change is as important as that we change. In a season of changeless change, the best of our traditions must accompany the best of the new technology (and praise songs are companions of silent prayers). As we move into this new world, it is vital that we understand what we must take with us.

Core and Circumference

Recently a poet suggested that the distinction between tradition and innovation is the difference between "core" and "circumference"—that is, we need to understand what is essential to our identity and what is not. Each tradition within the Christian church must be about this self-discovery. Is organ music a core reality, or is it circumference? Is a historically unbroken worship form core or circumference? Do chanting the liturgy and reading the prayers connect us to the core or to the circumference of our expressed faith?

For many, the answer to these and similar questions is to say that everything is core, a response that has led to the so-called worship wars and other nonsense. The worship wars have been waged in the name of purity. The core of worship was not simply that only one type of music was truly worshipful, but that certain actions had to be done in particular ways. This side of the altar was the correct place for these words; the other side, for that action. The best way to lead was to "dehumanize" the readings so that worship was not polluted by the personality of the leader—as if that could ever be possible!

Technique is not core because technique is never content. When technique becomes the point, the circumference has become the core. When everything matters, that which is truly valuable is lost in all the details. The "how" is confused with the "what."

Changeless change is a way of saying that the how must always serve the what. Change is appropriate when the change does not hide or get in the way of what that change is intended to communicate more adequately. When change gets in the way, then leave it alone. More to the point, when the traditional communicates the message best, the traditional is reintroduced with conviction and power.

Symbols have strength only when they are understood. When an eagle is seen as the embodiment of a nation, it is more than just a bird. When a cross is understood as symbolizing the love of God that would not hesitate to go the final mile for us so that we might have life, it becomes more than a piece of personal jewelry.

If Baptism and the Lord's Supper are moments when the divine touches human life in a particular way, then whatever music we employ to introduce and transition from these moments must serve that profound truth. The how serves the what!

Let the church truly become a learning organization. Learning organizations understand that mistakes are necessary to learning and that failure is a moment of grace. Such organizations are committed to a mission so valuable and compelling that innovation and excellence are assumed as necessary to achieve the goal. Risk must be rediscovered as a missional strategy for the church. Point A changes to point B only when we are compelled to assess our current reality honestly, to identify where we agree we must go, and then to risk getting there. There are no risk-free ministries. The only question is whether we will risk for the sake of the future or for the sake of the past.

4.
God's Future,
Our Mission

Point B: An eVective ministry in mission.
The event-horizon for the Christian church in the twenty-first century is its great future within the promises of our God. We have already discussed the cultural and church-wide context, our point A. While the data may seem depressing, nevertheless our Lord promises a future filled with possibility and transformation. At the very time when many of our leaders and ministries seem to lack vitality and vision, the voices of modernity and post-modernity are opening incredible doors for our witness.

Spiritual Awakening

We have already discussed the spiritual hunger of our times. Let me simply point out the explosion of spiritual perspectives on everything from business practice and success to personal change and self-help. Simply go into any bookstore and view the titles of many of our best-sellers. To top it off, one of the greatest minds of our time, Deepak Chopra, sells spirituality as a basis for a life that works. The newspapers and evening television are replete with references to the spiritual. A major change from the world in which the Protestant church thrived in North America, however, is that the Judeo-Christian basis for much of this "explosion" is lost in a soft spirituality in which anything goes. This is religion à la carte—religion without a doctrinal base. But the hunger for it is still both visible and very real.

Along with this unfocused spiritual awakening has emerged an interest in the divine within science. That which at one time seemed the foe that would undo theism in the West has begun to emerge as a surprising partner.

Leading physicists, among them John Barrow and Paul Davies, assert that twenty-first-century physics not only is compatible with a belief in a divine creator but that the best of science actually points to the existence of God as a necessity. This is partially because for our world and life as we know it to exist, certain realities must have taken place. An infinitesimal error of one to ten to the sixtieth power would have made this universe, as we know it, impossible. That is why astrophysicists such as Sir Fred Hoyle have asserted that any other conclusion is "obtuse."

At the other end of the scientific spectrum, such prominent biologists as Arthur Peacocke and Elving Anderson have made similar claims based on their understanding of evolution and its complexity. To these claims has been added the realization of the wonderfully complex aspects of genomes.

The intricacies of greater and lesser aspects of the universe continue to invite science and religion into a remarkable partnership of shared wonder. This shared sense of wonder indicates a basic purpose to creation and suggests not only a purposive, intelligent will at work but also a providence that works with and through human beings. I am not suggesting that science has finally proved the existence of God. Such arguments are self-serving and suspect. What I believe is absolutely true, however, is that the skepticism of modern science has given way to a more congenial attitude. This stance combines with the postmodern yearning for the spiritual to create a marvelous opportunity for faithful and fruitful witness. The Christian church need no longer remain silent before the caustic derision of those who claim science as the basis for dismissing our claims to an involved, benevolent, and intelligent will, which we know as God— specifically, the God made most clearly known in Jesus of Nazareth. And to those who suggest that postmodern spirituality does just fine without the concrete claims of this revealed God, we calmly point out our postmodern longing for conscience and a clear basis for morality and justice.

Imagine a Church . . .

Let the vision for the church be a return to bold but compassionate witness! Let our mission be nothing less than to change the world through changed lives! In other words, let us reassert the basic vision of our founder—to make passionate followers of Jesus Christ through the power of God's Holy Spirit and the Word.

God's future for the church is that each of its ministries would seek more clearly to embody the values and beliefs that we can identify from the Scriptures as those that exemplify the savior Jesus—his life, ministry, death, and resurrection. Such a future would indeed be worthy of our living it. The truth of the matter is that every day, each week of the year, countless individuals spend their lives for the sake of their vision of the church and its ministry. Many, however, have little clarity about what that vision truly is. Unfortunately, for many, the vision is of ministry that is dated and without power. We believe in a God who calls us to the best and expects us not to spend our lives for anything less. That God in Jesus of Nazareth calls us to spend our lives in sacrificial service is absolutely clear. Let us reengage Scripture and conversation with one another to more clearly identify "the best" to which the Holy Spirit calls us.

What would such a ministry, such lives, look like? Imagine a church in which opportunities to experience the presence of the risen Savior were identified as the number one goal of the ministry. Imagine a church where translating this gift of grace into daily life was priority number two. Then imagine the consequences for individuals and families who felt the spiritual compulsion to bring the invitation to others through word and deed.

Imagine congregations in which the sin of jealousy of other ministries was confessed and the discipline to reject jealousy regularly practiced. Imagine a ministry in which the value each of us has in Jesus Christ was tenaciously asserted for everyone—regardless of social, political, or religious standing. Imagine a world in which the Savior sat in on boardroom decisions of business, finance, politics, and social service organizations because his followers brought his presence in nonintrusive ways that began with a respect for others' opinions and invited honesty.

Imagine a world in which being a Christian was not

identified with being American—or Norwegian or Brazilian or any other nationality. Imagine a world in which being a Christian meant having others understand first our commitments to the Savior and, because of them, our commitments to humankind and God's creation.

Disciple-making ministries not only imagine this vision for Christ's church, they seek to partner with God in making it happen. Aligning the mission and ministry of the church presumes a vision toward which the mission will strive. Discipleship provides such a vision. When the vision is clear, then we can begin to realign our resources, identify our most precious values and fundamental beliefs, and form strategies to embody the vision in our world.

As Christians, we believe that such a vision will come only as God's will is done. This means that the tension between our hopes and dreams and the event-horizon of God's new world still exists. I am lobbying that we turn loose our passions, gifts, and energy toward that vision. Sin is always with us, yet we are a people who live in grace and work from grace. Sin and grace should not be an excuse for our failure to dream a new dream and work to find God's will in that dream.

The world is ripe for this old/new dream of ours.

Simply Complex

Using the spiral of life as metaphor continues to help us grasp the movements of our times. Now we move from simple to complex to simply complex.

There was a time when faith in Jesus Christ was understood as a fairly simple thing. In the New Testament, the word *faith* is almost always used to describe the simple trust of a person, family, or community in the saving power of Jesus. This definition of faith was, at times, attested to by the Holy Spirit in ways that other Christians, who almost always wanted to make it more complex than that, could see and accept. This is the phenomenon, for example, in Acts 10. The wonders of a dream, followed by Peter's faithful response, culminate in the fruitful falling of the Holy Spirit upon Cornelius's household through Peter's witness. Peter's response is a typical affirmation of this simple definition of faith: "Then Peter said, 'Can anyone withhold the water for baptizing these people who have received the Holy Spirit just as we have?'" (Acts 10:46-47).

Over the centuries, such a response became inconceivable. From a simple trust in God through Jesus Christ, the Christian church began to define faith in terms of a set of propositions. I am not arguing with these formulations; rather, I am suggesting that we moved from simple to complex. I am not even suggesting that such wasn't necessary. The hand of God was certainly at work, and we who believe in our time have received the witness of those who trusted through such a period of our history.

Now we are turning back into a period of simplicity—but it carries with it the complexity of our history. To be simply complex is both to affirm faith as a simple trust in the saving actions of God in Jesus of Nazareth and to recognize the value of doctrine.

Similarly, we have come into a time when, as the churches have become increasingly complex, our structures need to be simplified. The organizational charts of most churches today institutionalize ineffectiveness. They speak of a separation of spirit and business, for example, that does not exist. The complexities of active discipleship require organizations that "get out of the way" of living the faith.

By "get out of the way," I do not mean to say "let anything go." Far from it. I believe that our organizations must restructure to call, equip, and send believers into the world for the purposes described above in our imaginary world and church. That means that we must talk about God's future for the church as it interacts with all creation and humankind. It means that we must align our instructions—biblically, theologically, and practically— to serve this interaction that will, necessarily, happen most frequently outside of the church and its activities.

■□▢□▢■

"I resigned from the stewardship committee not because I do not support Christian stewardship but because I couldn't stand the waste of my time and ideas," commented the Christian lay leader. "When we discussed a possible program or event, we would always have to hold on it until the executive committee agreed to take it to the entire church council. If they all agreed, then we could go ahead. Do you have any idea what my business would be like if I had this kind of process in place? I'd be bankrupt . . . and I don't just mean financially. My best people would leave me. I'd be out of great ideas so fast your head would spin." He continued with a sigh and a shake of his head: "And I cannot believe that the church cannot do any better than this."

After a moment of silence, this fine Christian man looked at me sadly and said, "Pastor, that's why I left the committee. And that is why I won't serve on your church

council either. Until the church can either get out of the
way or help its members actually *do something*, I just find
it too frustrating."

My friend eventually left our congregation. With him
went a very sizable annual tithe—not to mention his special gifts.

Why can't simple trust in the Holy Spirit at work within
committed members of a congregation be exercised?
Why do we need the processes and practices that impede
leaders and followers from getting ministry done?

I recognize the need for appropriate boundaries, but I
believe the complex machinations of our churches provide unnecessary dikes and dams that impede the flow of
ministry, not helpful banks or boundaries for the river of
Christian service. Let the simple, straightforward need
determine the complexity or simplicity of the strategy for
any ministry response. Let our church boards establish
simple and necessary policies that serve the larger vision
of turning God's people loose for mission.

Discipleship Is the Goal

The problem is that we do not know where we are going.
When there is confusion about our destination, there will
always be systems in place that first say no rather than
yes. Without a clear understanding of our identity or purpose, we most frequently give in to our anxieties.

With discipleship as the single goal of ministry, shortcuts can be found and God's people can be turned loose. If
we can trust God at work in and through one another, we
can let go of control and work toward accountability. Control means doing it "my way." Accountability means get-

ting it done effectively, in keeping with our beliefs and values, and in ways that strengthen and advance the church.

■□■□■

"Pastor," a lay leader began, "we believe that it is time to establish a job-transition ministry at Prince of Peace. We are here to tell you about it and get any input you might have." He paused and then added with a smile: "Actually, we are here to get you to endorse the idea. We have all had experience with this and have visited a number of ministries in this area. We just need you to help us get started. We'll do the rest."

He then went on to outline their vision for a ministry that was part job placement, part support group, and part prayer group. I was amazed at the breadth of their vision as well as its practicality. They knew the need. They had both the personal and the professional experience necessary to succeed, and they agreed to keep me informed and work within a ministry area for ongoing accountability and reporting. The simple thing for me to do was to bless the ministry and get out of the way—which I did.

If the point is to connect God's gifted people with needs through effective ministry teams, then the simple gives way to a wonderfully complex system. The organizational lines go in many different directions, but they all lead to meeting needs and return to an accountability structure that is known to those in ministry.

When you know where you are going, shortcuts can be taken. This team of men and women took a shortcut for an important endorsement, freeing themselves to identify with a ministry area and do the work.

When you don't know what your goal is, then no route will get you there. If our goal had been lost in an organization of hoop jumping, that ministry would still be, at best, in the minds of those men and women. But the need was clear. Their vision for a ministry that met that need fit our mission and vision. They had the gifts that could take the simple and complex and transform them into the simply complex: a simple meeting of needs that could expand in increasingly complex relationships and interactions.

Focus

The key is focus.

Not long ago a mission-start pastor of another denomination interviewed me. He had heard of our ministry and wanted to discover how we had grown in effectiveness. At the end of an hour of questioning, he asked, "What two or three things keep pastors from succeeding in ministry?"

After a few moments of reflection, I replied, "I can think of two things in my observation that sabotage effective and faithful ministry more often than anything else: the lack of focus and the failure of courage to keep a focus identified."

The reality is that focus is required in ministry. So many "good" things for Christian leaders to do exist that we can get lost in pursuing first one, then another. And nothing really gets done. Most Christian leaders want to say yes more frequently than no. The problem is that if we say yes all the time, we really say no—because we rarely accomplish much!

A clear focus on the vision for a ministry, with a simple mission as the strategy to accomplish that vision, makes possible our saying no so that we can say yes to what truly matters. At a conference hosted by the Leadership Network, Jim Collins, coauthor of *Built to Last*, said, "Good is the enemy of best."[1] *Good is the enemy of best!* That means that we lose the best of our ministries when we pursue that which is only "good." How often in the church have we seen excellence compromised when we are willing to settle for simply being good at something? A crisp focus on excellence empowers us to say no to what is good for the sake of what is best.

It takes the courage of leadership to say no to the multiplicity of "goods" brought to our attention every day. Often, well-intentioned people who are passionate about these "goods" bring them to us. But if these goods dilute the clear focus for mission, then we must have the courage to articulate that, as good as the cause may be, it doesn't fit the focus of our ministry. When leaders are willing to exercise this courage, they equip other leaders within the organization to ask the mission and vision question (the focus question) on their own. This frees leaders from the distractions of making the decision to say no for the sake of a clear focus.

Momentum

This focus for ministry has the remarkable capacity to harvest the miracles of momentum. Momentum happens when more and more of our people understand the purpose of our ministry and then get involved to see that it happens. The more people who can articulate the mission and vision, the more excitement they generate. The more excitement, the more energy. The more energy—

when focused—the more gets done. When God's people see that ministry is actually being done, they see the miracle of the Holy Spirit in action. And they will give us more time and resources than we ever thought possible. This is not a pipe dream; it is happening all over our country in a wide variety of ministries and contexts.

Focus + the courage of leadership = momentum. How we get "focus" has to do with identifying outcomes. What are the outcomes that you desire for your particular ministry? If life change were an outcome, how would you know when it was happening? Perhaps there would be more adult baptisms. Maybe you would see an increase in the number of participants in ministry, the number of tithers, the number of those willing to talk about their faith and bring others to worship. Wouldn't it be wonderful to see families making different decisions for their time? Can you imagine teens choosing to form a Bible study group at school—on their own and equipped to do so by the church?

■□■□■

"Pastor, how do I get motivated?" This young man had come to see me after the sudden death of his father. We discussed his grief and the spiritual work the experience required. We discussed his family and his life circumstances. That is when he asked the question.

What is motivation if not our passion focused on a destination or goal worthy of our best efforts? This man, in his grief, had lost any sense of personal goal. The spiritual condition of ennui is the loss of passion because our goals seem insubstantial. The church calls us to the greatest of goals.

Heaven on Earth

The destination of the Christian church has often been identified as heaven. In the Bible, however, Jesus speaks of God's kingdom in such a way that heaven is ours here and now. This is true not in a final sense but in the very real sense of experiencing heaven as transforming hope that imbues daily life with an incredible value. Each life can be seen as an eternal investment by our creator. Life then becomes a sacred journey. The sacred journey has a clear "destination," and our mission is to live toward that destination each day. Heaven is a part of everyday experience for the disciple of Jesus Christ. Eternity is the shadow cast by the presence of Jesus in the daily living of his followers. This shadow has the potential to touch everything we do through the power of the Holy Spirit.

I saw the man standing with his sign at the stoplight: "Vet in need of food money. God bless you." I stared straight ahead. He passed me by and then stopped and just waited. No one in the long line of cars was willing to help or give him anything.

But I thought of all that I have . . . and all that he, obviously, didn't have. And I wondered what difference it would make in his life if I gave him some money. Then I realized that was the wrong question. The real question was what difference it would make in my life if I turned away. I had no control over what he would do with what little I would give him. But I had the God-given power to choose my response. So I rolled down my window and handed him a ten-dollar bill. When he thanked me, he said, "God bless you." And I knew that God already had.

Then the miracle happened. As I rolled up my window, he walked to the car behind me, and I saw a young couple rolling down their window to give him some money. The miracle wasn't the money. It was the shadow of heaven that created generosity where there hadn't been any. The miracle was a taste of heaven's perspective in my heart and, not surprisingly, it touched the hearts of others.

The mission of living every day as a Christian, as the very presence of Christ, imbues lives with value. In this case, by acknowledging the value of that man—without my need to have all my controlling questions answered—my own life received a wondrous boost of heavenly value. Valuing "the other" always has the capacity to create choice in the lives of others. In this case, that meant that those in the vehicles behind me suddenly saw that intersection, that person, and that sign differently. This is the best of both being and seeing Christ in all of life and especially in our interactions with others.

Only God can create such heaven-inspired moments. All God asks of us is a willingness to be open and to respond. Then God adds eternity to our meager efforts and transforms the moment for us and for those around us.

I find it fascinating that the most "heavenly minded" are almost always the most "earthly good." We need only look at Mother Teresa or St. Francis of Assisi. We need only look at Hans Nilsen Hauge, who, vilified as a pietist, was responsible for public education and social welfare in Norway. And what of Martin Luther King Jr. or Bishop Desmond Tutu? The power of a spiritual destination is its ability to touch the journey of life with purpose and power.

The path of discipleship is defined by how we walk the daily journey of life. Someone has said, "Life is so daily." I understand that to mean that life comes to us one day at a time. If we wait for heaven to come someday, we will miss it today!

I find it fascinating that the Gospels present a Jesus who made the most of each moment and each encounter. I believe our Lord could do this because he knew that in every meeting, in each moment, eternity comes like a seed encased in a shell. The seed is forever. The shell is now. What Jesus and the saints who have followed him have had the capacity to do is to open the shell and reveal the seed of forever within.

Heaven isn't "out there." Heaven is like the very air we breathe. It is so close to us that we don't see it or experience it unless we pause and take note. When we stop and listen to our breathing, or are forced to monitor our breathing through stress, we discover this life-giving reality of air—and it is always around us, always present to us, always there for us!

As we live, we define ourselves and our world. I do not know if that man was actually a vet or not. I don't know if he spent the money he received for food or something less wholesome. What I do know is that my day was defined by seeing him, acknowledging him, and helping him. That is how I want my life to be defined . . . and that is how I hope our world can be defined. That is how I hope to identify heaven as a daily presence available to me to change the moment instantly.

The question that Jesus is so often asked is this: what must I *do* to inherit eternal life? He seems to always take the question seriously. What I understand him to say is that we are simply to do what God puts before us. The daily path of life becomes the thing, the possibilities of heaven touching the earth or not. Often the simple act of kindness is left undone because of the complexities of our "need to know." The Good Samaritan did not need to know all there was to know about the man beset by robbers and left for dead. The Savior didn't need to know everything about the thief on the cross in order to welcome him into eternity. Simply do what is before you in such a way that your life could be defined by that deed . . . and your life would have been worth your living it.

5.
Leaders as Followers

When Lonny and Robin developed a vision statement for their business, they found that it reflected their faith naturally. The reference to God in the statement was an unconscious grounding in reality. They were shocked and dismayed when one employee in particular reacted to their reference to "God-given gifts."

"This is a business statement," he said. "God has nothing to do with it." Others raised the question in gentler terms: "Should we use God's name?" Or "This might offend people." Or "I smell a lawsuit." Or even more pointedly, "Using God is a statement. There is nothing wrong with it but it colors us a certain way."

Lonny and Robin thought about it and decided to keep it in the statement. The reference was an essential element in how they understood themselves and the world. It was not an attempt at being sectarian. Rather, it was a clear faith statement that God was involved in the giving of all their gifts and talents, as well as those of everyone else.

The opening paragraph of their business vision reads: "As we look to the future, we foresee a company that is first and foremost a leader in marketing communications.

Our leadership comes not from any one person but from the rich blend of skill and talents God has entrusted to each of us."

The one employee still didn't like it. In fact, he rejected the vision statement because of that faith reference. It was not surprising that in a short period of time, that employee chose to work elsewhere.

Every Leader Is First a Follower

The disciple of Jesus Christ is first of all a follower of the Savior. The follower of the Savior takes seriously Christ's presence in every sphere of life. More than that, the disciple understands that the teachings and expectations of Jesus stand over all of one's life. Lonny and Robin knew that. Their reference to God was much more than simply a nod in God's direction. It was a bold statement that God would be understood as a partner in their business and as the author of the resources they had been given.

Disciples of Jesus Christ give God credit for all God has given. We know that God "owns" it all. What we have is a gift. All we have is, ultimately, on loan. We are the stewards of this treasure we call life, and Jesus makes it clear that, as managers of God's gift of life, we shall be accountable for our use and development of it. The parable of the talents is but one example of this teaching of Jesus.

Disciples Are Inevitably Apostolic

The Christian church is sent into the frontier of unbelief for the sake of God's love for God's world. This is a risking love of truth, compassion, and hope.

What Lonny and Robin stumbled into was a necessary outcome of their followership of the Savior. Followers of Jesus Christ engage the world in witness and welcome. The term *apostolic* defines this external engagement of the world in Jesus' name, which disciples naturally do sooner or later. The reason that Robin and Lonny "stumbled" into it rather than anticipating it is a significant cultural shift called pluralism. We are all aware of pluralism in our society. For some of us, it is a positive reality; for others, negative. Regardless, pluralism is here to stay. Most of us are surprised, however, when we run into it personally like Robin and Lonny did.

■□■□■

"How many of you have young children in public school?" I asked. Many hands went up. "Please keep your hands up, if you will." I said. Then, scanning this group of several hundred pastors and lay leaders from many congregations in the Upper Midwest, I said, "If you assume that your Christian values and beliefs will be supported by your public school, please leave your hand up."

I have asked this question in countless locations around the United States. The response is always just like that of the group I addressed above. All but one or two of the hands go down.

The point of the question is not to join those who trash public education! The point is that pluralism affects us unconsciously all the time. But most of us, like Robin and Lonny, don't give it much thought. In fact, we are surprised when we meet it personally. Disciples will unconsciously engage the world in ways that reflect their followership of Jesus of Nazareth. This engagement is the touch point of our witness and welcome to the love of God.

For years, pastors and theologians have said that there is no distinction between sacred and secular for the Christian. This has been a nice idea, but it has had little impact on the life of Christians overall—until now, that is. Discipleship compels an apostolic engagement that is a natural outgrowth of following Jesus. The lines between church and the world are blurred. The previously normal distinction between what was sacred and what was secular simply has no real-life application. For the disciple, as indicated in the previous chapter, every moment and each encounter carries the sacred. The only question is whether we will be open to it. There will be times, as with Lonny and Robin, when we will be surprised by the collision between our faith and the world.

When Prince of Peace initiated an outreach service at our local YMCA, our intent was to reach out to the larger community. We called it the JYM gathering: Jesus, You, and Me. Specifically, we thought we might engage persons of color from the apartment complexes near the Y or the many young adults in townhouses and condominiums near us. The result was a laboratory for worship and exercise.

But the greatest opportunity to emerge from the JYM gathering was an invitation to visit low-income housing developments in our community. This led to an initiative in the Stone Grove apartment complex. Through our Mission and Outreach Team, we became present through a variety of activities. The underlying principle was our commitment to evangelism and justice simultaneously.

We were surprised when the city administration invited us to partner at Stone Grove. Why? Because we made it clear that our witness to Jesus Christ was an essential element in any activity in which we engaged and, thus, that our presence would be linked to our witness. They agreed.

The beauty is that, at the same time, our witness achieved greater authenticity for us. Because we are a discipleship community of faith, we know that our apostolic engagement of the world must be through both word and deed. This is the blurring of the lines that have otherwise separated the evangelical from the social gospels. Apostolic communities, however, know that word and deed have always been one and the same.

The apostolic call is to live "outside of ourselves." By that I mean that disciples are prepared to be engaged by the world and to connect with the world. Ours is both a strategic and an opportunistic faith. It is strategic in that we look for ways to bring our faith and our service together as often as possible. It is opportunistic because we must always be open to the surprises that God will bring to us through the world. So we live beyond ourselves in extending our spiritual lives into the world God loves as well as leaning into the Spirit, who meets us as we engage God's world.

Know Your Followership Style

As a psychologist, Mark often cares for people in difficulty. Their problems may stem from their immediate circumstances or from long-term family of origin issues. He is both a compassionate and a skilled therapist. One of the questions that Mark will often ask his clients is, How does your faith help you in this? He is open to any response. Most frequently, the question opens the door to conversation about God's presence in times of difficulty and pain. Occasionally, the client rejects the question—and Mark moves on. Mark's followership style is caring and invitational. It may or may not lead to a conversation that is explicitly spiritual, let alone Christian.

What is a "followership style"? A simple definition is this: how we live in community and ground what we do in the practices of discipleship. Some styles are active; others, responsive.

Nancy Lee serves as pastor of children and family ministries. Not long ago, two women asked to see her. She agreed, and they came with a request to help create a mother-daughter retreat. With Nancy Lee's approval, a team was formed. Says Nancy, "My job was to work with the mothers on two aspects of the retreat. The first was the content and timing of the retreat. The second was to constantly call us back to 'The Marks of Discipleship' as the framework for our community life as followers of Jesus."

Nancy Lee's followership style was responsive in this situation. She responded to an identified need within the community and grounded it in our culture of discipleship. Mark's style is more proactive. He invites his clients to place their issues or situations within a spiritual context. The invitation can be accepted or rejected, but it is made out of Mark's commitment to follow Jesus Christ.

From Thinking to Perceiving to Sensing
(LOOP #6: THE DISCERNMENT LOOP)

The followership style of disciples who understand their apostolic call will probably be a combination of both situations described above. This style can be illustrated by another loop in life: from thinking to perceiving to sensing.

Consider how following is like a dance. When learning a dance, we first have to think about how to do it. We need to watch others and copy their steps. This requires *thinking*. We watch, we think our way through the movements, and then we practice those steps. But this isn't dancing.

The next stage in learning to dance is to move from thinking to *perceiving*. After the steps have been learned, we perceive the movement of the music and our partner. This process is external to us as we watch and anticipate. We are beginning to dance.

Real dancing occurs when we can let go into the *sensing* of the rhythm and melody. The music is no longer simply external to us. It enters us, and we seem to be carried away by it. The movement of the music is mirrored in the movement of our bodies and is unconsciously communicated to our partners.

When disciples consciously engage the world with their following of Jesus Christ clearly in mind, it is often like dancing. The first occasions are difficult. For Mark, his first exploration into the faith realm of therapy was a conscious decision. He worked to frame the question in a respectful and open-ended manner that would allow clients to reframe the question in a way that might be helpful for them. It was not about Mark imposing his own experience or theology on the other. Rather, the question served to invite the other to place the personal situation within a bigger context that included faith and, presumably, God. Only much later did this question become a natural and easy part of the relationship between client and therapist, as well as the other spiritual questions Mark now habitually asks.

We have come through a time when structures and institutions were created to form the interface between the Christian and the world. Structures and institutions require thinking. The form of the organization is external to us. For us to create the structure, we need to think about it as an external thing, which allows us to form it according to its necessary function. We have learned that form and function are much more dynamic processes than this externalizing would suggest. Form follows function until the form is in place. Then form itself shapes the function.

So our culture began to demand more responsiveness from our institutions, a situation that has been especially true of our churches and ministries. As this expectation clearly emerged, our concepts of effective organizations shifted to require an institutional perceiving of the world, the function for which it was formed, and whether or not that form was helpful.

This major shift occurred through the speed and magnitude of change. The faster the speed of perceiving and responding and the greater the magnitude of change required, the more we moved from perceiving to sensing. Organizations no longer have the time to think, then perceive, and then act. Mobile organizations must make the move to sensing—just like dancing.

Perhaps our churches are most frequently resistant to this looping in life. Ministry has become hostage to structure. An opportunity for launching a new ministry surfaces, and by the time the necessary steps have been taken to wade through our structure, the opportunity is gone. Or someone presents an idea for greater effectiveness in ministry. After months of processing the idea, the individual's passion has waned or the person has become frustrated and has left.

Structures are necessary, and thinking is necessary. But responding to the spiritual possibilities of our time will not always allow the time for jumping through institutional hoops. We need to incorporate the dance of leadership in our churches and allow for the freedom of sensing and responding to opportunities and ideas that fit within the mission and vision of our churches.

■❑❚❑■

"My constitution hasn't been approved either," he said. We were a group of senior pastors of large churches discussing both our loyalty to our denomination and our frustrations. Of the pastors at that table, with a combined discipleship number of twenty-five thousand members or more, none of us had a constitution that had been approved by our denomination. The level of financial support for the denomination was in the millions . . . and waning. Why? Because the denomination was increasingly perceived as blocking rather than supporting effective and innovative ministry.

Denominations must stop being "regulatory agencies." Appropriate vision and mission can be established in a manner that sets healthy boundaries for affiliation with a denomination. But the lockstep requirements for constitutional clauses and structural adoption make little sense in this age of mission. For denominations to survive, they too must move from thinking to perceiving to sensing.

The real question for leaders in the church is, Where do you *sense* the Spirit is leading your ministry? This question suggests that Christian leaders must be grounded in the practices of spiritual discernment. Spiritual discernment springs from prayer and Scripture. From there it engages the world through observation, critique, and need (or opportunity) assessment. This leads to seeking the leading of the Holy Spirit, a sensing distilled through the culture of the church. The last step in this discernment process is testing: thinking, perceiving, and challenging the actions taken and their consequences.

This is mission at work. Structures and institutions must be created to encourage and embody this discernment process.

Know Your Followership Values

Such openness to the Holy Spirit requires that we know our followership values. These values spring from the leaders' understanding of what it means to be a follower of Jesus Christ. Such values are identified by the church and forged in the crucible of real life. They begin in the gift of certainty that the gospel declares. Those who have been called into faith by the power of the Holy Spirit are invited to the certainty of God's grace and eternal life. This confidence allows us to reposition ourselves.

■□■■□■

"But if we make our witness to Jesus more obvious, won't we be less welcoming to those who aren't Christian in our community. Our C.D.L.C. (Child Development and Learning Center) has always had a policy of welcoming everyone—no matter what their faith may or may not be."

Our director was raising a key point. If we are clear about our faith and confidence in Jesus Christ, will we be less open to those who do not share our religious convictions?

"My experience and conviction is that those who have the greatest confidence in that which they believe are the most open and the least threatened by those who do not share their beliefs," I replied. "Not only that but, since C.D.L.C. is housed in and related to Prince of Peace, most if not all of those who bring their children here expect us to reflect our faith. We need to do that— but in a manner that is respectful of others' beliefs. I know we can do that."

One year later, only one family had withdrawn from this remarkable program. Others were grateful for the clarity of our witness and purpose, even those whose beliefs were markedly different from ours.

Confidence of faith allows us to reposition ourselves. The question is whether our faith is a fortress or a springboard into life and the world. The problem with a fortress mentality for faith is that the only difference between a fortress and a prison is who holds the keys. Life has a way of turning the fortress of faith into a prison within which we must defend ourselves from the very world that Jesus Christ came to save. So we turn from the opportunities of mission and service to surviving under siege. Such a perspective is absent from the New Testament church.

Followership values that are established in the confidence of our faith in Jesus Christ create an openness to engage the world in honesty, care, and conviction. The honesty of our faith often translates into authenticity. Christian leaders who hide behind a perfectionist model are suspect in our time. This doesn't mean that we "air our dirty laundry." Rather, Christian leaders can share their vulnerability and struggles in healthful ways that engage others. When leaders speak of such a real faith, it invites others into an open conversation about and with God.

This honesty is translated institutionally when we are open about why we are engaged in service or ministry. When others know our purpose, they become less suspicious of our care. Convictions are like light—that is, they were never intended to be hidden beneath a blanket of social anxiety. Rather, with social sensitivity, we will make our convictions known when the opportunity is provided.

From Answers to Questions to Answering Questions
(LOOP #7: THE LOOP OF SPIRITUAL RESPECT)

This leads us to another looping of our world. The church has positioned itself as an institution of answers and, in fact, we have some significant answers to give. But our world has moved from a passive willingness to listen to answers to a more interactive learning. From the confidence we have in Jesus Christ, the church can move to engaging the world first through questions, not simply by stating answers.

Recently, we created a worship series and secured a domain site named e-doubts.org. The purpose of the series was to honestly engage in the questions that people had about the Christian faith. These questions would be addressed from the simple basis of the Apostles' Creed. The interesting thing was how that process of moving from answers to questions opened us as a believing staff to greater dialogue and interaction. The questions led to Scripture. The Scripture then created a foundation for answering questions.

Margaret Wheatley has suggested that beneath the cultural propensity of people taking offense is the *need to be seen*. Speaking at a Leadership Network conference in May 2000, Wheatley urged church leaders "to enter into the willing suspension of being offended." She further suggested that, if we are willing to refuse to be offended, we could find one another. "The way to find each other is through the simple human act of listening to each other."[1]

Wheatley is simply suggesting that Christians become less addicted to our answers and more open to the questions of our time. When we are willing to shift to "answering questions," we will be much more open to listening. This listening will empower us to find one another.

As I read the Gospels, I am struck by how often Jesus simply stops in order to hear or to see someone. This leads the Savior to *ask questions* that we would have so easily ignored in order to give an answer we would assume to be good for that person.

For example, in Mark we read of Jesus' going through Jericho. As Jesus is surrounded by his disciples and a large crowd, his purpose clearly leading him to Jerusalem, blind Bartimaeus cries out to him. Those around the blind man tell him to be silent, but he shouts out louder. When Jesus stops and asks others to bring Bartimaeus to him, Jesus asks the question "What do you want me to do for you?" (Mark 10:51).

Jesus asks this question in order to truly see and hear. So, too, Christian leaders must honor the questions themselves and not simply see in them another opportunity to declare an answer. This looping is a remarkable opportunity for mission and for making the truth and witness of the gospel both clear and relevant.

While attending graduate school in psychotherapy, I remember hearing a professor tell us, "The first hundred hours, you will probably do more harm than good. But those hundred hours are necessary in order for you to become capable and truly helpful. And remember, the presenting issue—that is, the issue for which a person seeks you out—is rarely the real one. But if you do not respond respectfully and effectively to that issue, you'll never get to what really matters."

The church is like that. If we put our answers in front of the questions of our time, we will never get to what truly matters. The church must stop, take seriously those around us, and then dare to ask the question in order to get to what really matters in the followers' lives. The looping from answers to questions to answering questions makes this possible. To paraphrase Margaret Wheatley, it involves a willing suspension of assuming we already know what the world needs and how they need it.

Know Your Followership Boundaries

In Acts 10, Peter has a paradigm-bursting vision. A canopy descends from the sky, and all manner of nonkosher animals and insects are on the canopy. The voice from heaven declares, "Get up, Peter; kill and eat," to which Peter, that faithful kosher Jew, replied, "By no means, Lord; for I have never eaten anything that is profane or unclean." Then the voice declares, "What God has made clean, you must not call profane."

The vision was a spiritual preparation for Peter to break the kosher laws by going with gentile servants, entering into the gentile home of Cornelius, and worshiping with him and his household. Peter's willingness to sense the leading of the Spirit and follow it created new boundaries for his ministry that he would not fully understand until much later.

As expansive as the new boundaries for Peter were, they were also clearly defined. Peter did not go to just any gentile home. He went to Cornelius's home. Peter did not immediately worship with Cornelius. He worshiped with Cornelius's household in baptism only after the Spirit made it clear that the Word had borne the fruit of faith. And later, he would explain what he had done by articulating these very boundaries.

In our time, the question for followers of Jesus Christ is not how to do good. The opportunities for doing good are so great that they can be incapacitating. Every week, Christians receive pleas for involvement and funding from many legitimate and compassionate organizations. Many of these groups have sprung from within the Christian faith; many originate outside of a faith context.

Leaders know that we cannot respond to all of them. We cannot do all the good that is asked of us.

Peter is instructive here. Followership boundaries mean accepting the limitation of being human. We seek to respond to those to whom the Spirit calls us. How do we discern that call? First, if we have no passion for it, the Spirit most likely is not calling us to it. Second, if we have no particular gifts to bring to the endeavor, it is probably not an invitation by the Spirit. Lastly, if we cannot see how we can make a significant impact, then it is probably not the specific opportunity to which we are called. In other words, it's not Cornelius's house, and we shouldn't experience guilt for saying no.

Institutionally, this process is part of the discernment process mentioned earlier. Such a process must always be placed within the particular calling of a particular ministry. If the opportunity doesn't fit within the mission, vision, and values of the ministry, it should not be done.

Followership boundaries are necessary for the focus and momentum discussed in chapter 4. Proceeding without boundaries compromises our effectiveness significantly because we will try to do too much too often. We succumb to the temptation to be busy but do not necessarily accomplish much.

It's Not Just about Us

Ministry is about the one we follow and those who follow us. If a ministry opportunity presents itself and no one shows up or no leader steps forward, that is a clear indication that the Spirit is not calling us to act at this time or in this place. If a leader feels compelled to act on the opportunity anyway, then it leads to other questions: Is this a personal rather than community calling? Is this the community in which the leader is still called to lead?

Most of us have experienced "failures" in ministry, and most of us assume that we were somehow to blame for their lack of success or effectiveness. But if it is not just about us, something else may be going on. It may be a mismatch between need and gifts. It may simply be the wrong time. Or it may be that the leader is out of step with the followers. It's like dancing: if the leader is doing the waltz and the followers are doing the tango, it just won't work! The leader must ask herself whether she is willing to spend more time doing the tango in the hope that she can lead the followers into a waltz at a later date. Only the leader can determine the call of the Spirit in such circumstances and discern the boundaries of the call. After all, when Peter had baptized Cornelius and his household, he left. His mission had been accomplished. He had reached the boundaries of his time with that gentile household.

6.
Resourcing Your Ministry

"I don't know if I am really called to stay here much longer." The pastor was serving in a small town. The congregation had grown under her leadership, but she and her husband had always seen themselves in a metropolitan setting. She was now engaged with her leadership in a visioning exercise, and she knew that to proceed she needed to make a long-term commitment to this ministry. Without that commitment, she could not invite her congregation into a vision for the future with her leading. It was a matter of trust, and she knew it. No wonder her ministry had borne such fruit.

Trust Is the Currency of Ministry

The bank account of ministry is not the church treasury. Rather, it is in the hearts of those the church serves. Trust is the currency for ministry. The higher the level of trust, the more effective that ministry will be. The greater level of trust in the leadership of the church, the more willing God's people are to enter into mission—that is, to change for the sake of the gospel of Jesus Christ.

One reason the pastor in the above story was effective was that she was unwilling to be less than clear about her commitment to the congregation. The conversation we had was not public, but it was an insight into the integrity with which she engaged ministry. Those whom our churches serve intuitively sense such spiritual integrity. In fact, I believe that the people of God are remarkably patient and accepting when they have a significant level of trust in their church. This pastor was unwilling to betray that trust by leading her congregation in a vision process to which she could not give her own commitment. Her personal struggle was necessary to enable the correct decision as to whether the process ought to continue and, if so, how.

There was a time when leaders could assume a level of trust (or followership) out of respect for their role. That age has passed. Now, after an increasingly brief honeymoon, leadership must earn and reclaim trust again and again. Fundamental to this process is the commitment of the leader to those whom he serves. If the trust level of a ministry is low, one key question is, How committed is the leader to his or her followers? In other words, how trusting is the leader of the followers?

One of the most effective ways to inspire trust is to give it. The more controlling a leader is, the less his or her followers will feel trusted. The less trusted followers feel, the less they are willing to extend trust to the leader.

"Then Jesus called the twelve together and gave them power and authority over all demons and to cure diseases, and then sent them out to proclaim the kingdom of God and to heal. He said to them, 'Take nothing for your journey, no staff, nor bag, nor bread, nor money—not even an extra tunic. Whatever house you enter, stay there, and leave from there. Wherever they do not welcome you, as you are leaving that town shake the dust off your feet as a testimony against them.' They departed and went through the villages, bringing the good news and curing diseases everywhere" (Luke 9:1-6).

The interesting intersection of this text with our conversation is the level of trust that Jesus gave the twelve. Jesus gave them power and authority. He then commissioned them and gave them remarkable instructions that told the twelve they would be provided for and that they were capable. The text rather sparsely records the response of the twelve: "They departed . . ."

In other words, they got it. They had come to trust Jesus and believed that he would not send them out to fail or to become wounded unnecessarily. His confidence in them was an affirmation of their confidence in him.

Leaders in the church who recognize that trust is the real currency of ministry know that, sooner or later, they will need to empower their followers with trust. The currency of ministry cannot be hoarded. In fact, the more it is shared, the more it grows.

God's People Are Our Greatest Resources

Again, let me return to an event mentioned earlier. I knew these three: two men and a woman. They had been involved in our ministry for years. Now they were proposing the launching of a new ministry for job seekers. They had visited at least one site in our metropolitan area that hosted a long-standing and acclaimed ministry to connect job seekers with possible employers, and they were pitching the idea to me. Did I think it would work? Would I, as senior pastor, be willing to support it publicly?

The economy was already faltering, and in the aftermath of the horrific events of September 11, 2001, the number of layoffs and cutbacks was shocking. "What a great idea," I exclaimed. "And I think the timing couldn't be better. But you don't need me. Just go for it! And of course I will support it when you need me to. But it's your mission. . . . Just do it."

I then referred them to the appropriate staff person for support and trusted that, if they were serious and the Spirit blessed it, this ministry was off and running. And it was! The response in our community and from the press was tremendous. The team these three created continues to grow.

God's people are the church's greatest resource! This ministry idea was entirely theirs. I was aware of the need but had no time or energy to direct toward meeting it. They, along with a growing team, experienced the prompting of God's Spirit and followed it. They researched the alternatives already available, sifted through the positives and negatives of launching the ministry, and brought it forward.

That was the point when I had to get out of the middle. Though they were clearly called and gifted, they felt the need to inform and involve the pastor. I knew that I could very easily step into the middle of this ministry and that the result would be that I would (1) slow the ministry down, (2) become frustrated at the time demands it would make on me, and (3) by my involvement withhold the trust that fuels our ministry.

My first task was to listen and to ask how this new ministry fit within our mission and vision. Once it was clear that they saw that link, my second task was simple: refuse to allow them to "delegate it up." By that I mean that I needed to affirm that it was their ministry and calling, not mine. More than that—and this is the difficult part— they didn't need me.

It is one thing to say (and believe!) that we can trust our people. It is quite another to give up my need to be needed. Codependency is one of the great sins of the church. Christians know the command of Christ to care for others. Our obedience to this command can very easily take the form of my serving my own need to be needed at the expense of those whom I would serve. The ministry of God's church does not exist for me or from me. The Christian church comes from God and exists for the sake of the world that God loves. The Holy Spirit comes to empower Christians in the gospel. We are truly blessed in order to continue God's blessing through us in the world. Part of continuing that blessing is turning the called loose to become involved in ministry according to their gifts and passions.

The task is both to trust God and to trust God at work through God's people. Time and time again, the church has created structures that belie this fundamental principle. In the story from Luke above, we see Jesus modeling this very trust for us. Jesus Christ does not ask perfection of us. He asks only for obedience and effort. Let the Christian church through its leaders expect no less—nor anything more.

Changed Lives Create a Changing Church

I opened the envelope and found a two-thousand-dollar check inside. I read the note enclosed and felt my heart leap. I knew this woman. I didn't know much about her living circumstances, but I knew that she had two small children, brought them to Sunday school and worship regularly, and now attended our in-depth Bible study. In her note, she expressed her profound gratitude for all that our church was doing for her and her children. I wondered how she could afford a contribution this size.

Later, we met in my office. I found that she is a single mother whose life has been transformed by the gospel of Jesus Christ. She had received a large check and felt called to give to the ministry that means so much to her and her children. She wrote the check with great joy, she said. It was 40 percent of the check she had received!

There are times when Christians are truly humbled by the generosity of others. This was such a moment for me. We prayed together, thanked God together, and knew the presence of Jesus in my office.

Changed lives necessarily will change the church. Lives touched by the power of the Holy Spirit are more generous than we could ever imagine. This generosity is in spirit as well as in time and resources. In fact, I have never met a truly generous person who hasn't had a life-changing encounter with God in one way or another. We in the Christian church have the possibility of being a spiritual catalyst for such mystical encounters. We will know them most frequently after the fact. That was the privilege of meeting with her in my office. I caught a glimpse of the footprints of God on the sands of her life.

Perhaps part of our inability to really trust God at work in his people is because we have forgotten the real power of the gospel. Life in the church can be so *daily*. The routines and rhythms can lull us into a state of normalcy in which the miraculous can get lost in the blur of the usual.

But every now and then, the Spirit of the living God grants us a glimpse of God's ongoing work in our midst. That is what happened with the note, the woman, and, least of all, the check.

We live and work to our expectations. In education, we have found that students who face limited expectations of their academic performance produce at that level. Those students who are challenged will, barring insurmountable limitations, rise to the level of those expectations. The question for us as disciples of Jesus Christ is, How high are your expectations? Do we expect God to be at work in and through us or not? If we do, then let's look for the miracles and, when we see them, claim them for the glory of the one we serve and follow.

Heart and Hands Follow Our Identified Treasure

Jesus teaches: "Where your treasure is, there your heart will be also" (Matthew 6:21).

I have been told that at the time of Christ, the heart was the seat of both the emotions and the will. If so, then Jesus is telling us the truth about our lives when he says that where our identified treasure is, that is where we make the real choices of life. It is there also that we feel or experience life to the fullest.

The treasure for that remarkable woman had become the church. Her hands and heart followed that treasure.

How can we work so that the treasure of the church can replace the institution of the church? Perhaps we can best approach the possibilities through three questions.

1. What is the primary outcome of our ministries? Is it that people should *know* Christ or that they should know *about* Christ? The primary invitation of our relational God is that we know God. Christians believe that the coming of the incarnate Christ was born out of this eternal impulse in the heart of our creator. The secondary invitation is that we know about God. The Scriptures, in the church of this age, will be viewed first as an invitation to come and know God and then, second, as documents that inform our knowledge about God. The spiritual hunger of our time is not for knowledge. We are on knowledge overload! The spiritual hunger is for a relationship with the living God. The knowing of God unlocks the treasure of Christ's church to us.

2. Are Christians called to wear a cross or to carry the cross? The difference is monumental. Wearing a cross like a piece of jewelry costs little. Carrying a cross costs much. To carry our cross is to be willing to witness in word and deed to the Crucified One. We do not flee the cost of ridicule or embarrassment. We are willing to risk failure and defeat for the sake of spiritually changed lives. We are eager to adapt to our time and culture, unless such adaptation compromises the reign of Christ. Again, it is a clear understanding that it isn't really about us: our comfort, our timetable, our claim to the right forms and language.

Wearing a cross tames the untamable. Perhaps one of the gifts of our time has been the "secularizing" of the cross as jewelry. Just because a person wears a cross doesn't mean that the person carries one.

I am not suggesting that Christians ought not wear crosses! I do myself. Rather, I am suggesting that the church—and especially its leaders—know the critical difference. One is a nice gesture. The other is a life of risk for the sake of the gospel. One unlocks the treasure of the church. The other is simply a nice shape.

3. Are we following Jesus of Nazareth for the sake of recognition or for responsibility? Responsibility is a foreign concept for many of us in the twenty-first century. Responsibility is a commitment for the sake of another. Recognition is my commitment for the sake of myself.

I recognize that we cannot always differentiate these two, but such a distinction is critical for discovering the treasure of the church. From this clarity can come the renewing process of confession, forgiveness, and new beginnings. Recognition lasts only as long as the moment. Responsibility for the gospel is as timeless as the promise of eternal life.

Resourcing ministry is, first, relationship building. The primary relationship is between the believer and Christ. The second relationship is between how the follower of Jesus relates to the world. Christ has chosen the church to be the primary vehicle for that relationship. With no apologies, then, we should be serious about harvesting the abundance of God for the sake of Christ's church. God has provided for us through God's people and the trust that makes ministry possible.

What about Money?

Money isn't the real deal. Relationship is. Vision is. Mission is. Money follows.

Four piles of ministry resources and expenditures exist. The first is in operations, which include all the necessary expenditures for the ongoing accomplishment of our ministry. If people are our number one resource, then we should see the largest pile of expenditures in people areas: staff and programs.

"I can't believe that we spend nearly 60 percent of our budget on staff," he said. "In my business, I wouldn't tolerate that! We've got to get our staff costs under control."

"You're wrong," she said. "The staff is our ministry. They make possible not only the programming of this church but also, and more importantly, the training and deploying of people. I think spending nearly 60 percent of our budget on staff costs is a good deal!"

With the DNA model as a metaphor for a new approach to the problem, we can ask the question: Who is right? The answer: both are. The need for staffing for ministry is clear to most of us, but so is the need for clear accountability. The man's context above couldn't tolerate a cost-of-position ratio like that in the church. On the other hand, such an expenditure for people to *do the ministry* rather than to *equip and send others* in ministry would also be unacceptable. Staff time should be spent replicating themselves: growing others in the depth of their faith-lives and then turning them loose in ministry. This is the multiplication principle of the gospel. This is how five loaves and two fish could feed five thousand! This grows resources, while the old way simply spends resources. Churches that invest dollars in key staff who support and equip others for ministry can expect the abundance of God to become more available to them.

The second pile is capital expense. Investment in buildings and grounds will eventually be necessary. The care for facilities is simply a requirement of good stewardship. Yet churches frequently allow time and use to beat up the physical resources for their ministries. Perhaps there was a time when this was acceptable. If so, that time has ended. Few people are willing to spend significant time in buildings and on grounds that are inferior to their own homes. Again, the need to manage such resources requires an unashamed providing for them. When people discover the treasure of the church, their desire to give God the best will also move them to upgrade and care for the place from which ministry and mission move.

The third pile is mission. The Christian church has always been called to give for mission. In 2 Corinthians 8 and 9, we get an insight into this call in the early church. The expectation was twofold: first, that the believers would tithe in their weekly service of worship and thus provide for their local mission, and second, that they would give over and above that tithe for the sake of extraordinary need. In the case cited in 2 Corinthians, such giving was to provide for the Jerusalem church in a time of famine.

Mission expenditures should include both. The weekly tithe is the invitation to reach out in faithful mission in the community as well as globally. But there also are extraordinary events to which Christians will want to respond in a special manner. After the events of September 11, 2001, many churches took up special offerings. In the long run, these offerings will multiply themselves because the perceived integrity of the Christian church as a group of believers who give beyond themselves will be enhanced. Other events that might require such an offering include natural disasters or a community's or family's sudden and clear need. When the church responds to these events, the heart of the church, the treasure of God's people as a giving people, grows.

The fourth pile is for long-term investment, the foundation or endowment that many churches are building. Those who give to these expressions of the ministry do so in the hope that they will help build a legacy of effective witness and care through the church that has been a treasure to them. The accountability for such money should be (1) to spend it in keeping with the donor's request (or give it back) and (2) to use it to increase the effectiveness of the church's mission for the future.

Though we have spoken of these resources and expenditures in terms of "piles," they are more accurately passions. People give to their passions, and when the church becomes a vehicle for passionate giving, the hearts of others are opened to the joy of giving. To the degree possible, effective ministries do two things: (1) they refuse gifts that simply don't fit their vision, mission, and unique culture, and (2) they connect giving to the passion of those who give. This makes clear the connection between treasure and heart. Once that connection is made, it is remarkable how the heart becomes more open to other opportunities for giving.

7.
Managing
the Change

People do not change because they want to. Rather, they change because they discover they must. Dr. Mark Zipper, vice president of change management for Allina Health Systems, cites as an example of this truth the "burning platform" story of Royal Dutch Shell Company. Royal Dutch Shell had a hard-and-fast rule that, while working on an oil rig in the North Sea, under no circumstances were the workers to jump into the water. The waters were so cold and the chance of rescue so remote that the rule was for the crew's safety. One day, a fierce fire erupted on one of the rigs and, contrary to the rule, some of the crew jumped into the frigid waters below. Of those that jumped, some survived. They were the only survivors of the fire.

After an appropriate length of time for the survivors to recover, officials of Royal Dutch Shell interviewed them and asked why they had jumped. To a person, they replied simply, "The platform was on fire. To stay was certain death. At least if we jumped, we stood a chance."

"Managing change begins with a burning platform," Dr. Zipper asserts.[1] The burning platform is that set of circumstances that makes the change necessary. Managing change begins by seeing the burning platform and then making it visible to those through whom the change must come.

Persistence = Patience + Purpose

Making the circumstances that necessitate change visible to others requires persistence. Most people respond to the assertion of such circumstances with denial. "The platform isn't really on fire," they will contend.

Churches and church leaders have been in denial of the need for change for some time. That denial began to crack in most Protestant denominations in the United States about a decade ago. The denial was challenged as the denominational losses continued unabated. In sheer numbers of persons, the losses of the past decade are unprecedented. Yet history was the most often articulated reason not to change.

That is the second phrase of denial: "We've had fires before. This one is no different. We'll soon put it out."

After a decade of evangelism, one such denomination reported at its national assembly the outcomes of its ten years of study. The decline had lessened to 4 percent, the numbers of "in trouble" congregations and clergy remained about the same, and "we know much more about evangelism than we did before."[2] The report presented recommendations to help that church move forward, but the underlying confidence was that the "fire" on the platform of the church would be put out over time.

Substantive change was still around the corner. Persistence was the only way forward.

Persistence is not simply patience. Patience waits, whereas persistence waits while it acts. Persistence continues to declare the platform on fire. More than that, persistence begins to change the pieces in place—or at least to plan for their change. This is patience with a purpose. The outcome is clear: change is necessary for the survival of a vital church.

The second step in managing change is to plan for that change by imagining what must be changed. In the looping metaphor, this means to imagine how seeming opposites can be harmonized. The past becomes a platform from which we must jump, but it is not the place we shall land. This is the stage of managing the perceived and actual losses of the change.

■□■□■

"I loved the church I grew up in," she said. "It was a wonderful congregation in which we all knew one another, or thought we did. And the pastor chanted the liturgy while the organ played the hymns my grandmother and I would sing together. I loved that church. But it doesn't exist anymore. They closed it down a few years ago."

This Christian woman was expressing her loss. The loss was real. It was the loss of intimacy and tradition. One interesting aspect of the story is that she had moved away from that church years before and joined a thriving congregation with a contemporary look and feel. "It's the one my children want to attend," she said succinctly.

Other losses can be just as real. But notice what remained. What she still had was a ministry that brought her family together, just as that other church had done but for a different generation. Change always means loss. The question is whether the platform is burning hot enough for the loss to be considered necessary. The process of managing change respects such losses and then focuses on what has been brought from the past into the present for the sake of the future good.

In speaking of the need for change, leaders often make the mistake of using language that matters to them but doesn't matter to those who must make the change. If, in the example above, the woman could see that change was necessary in order to include her children in another generation of worshiping Christians, her loss could be put within an acceptable emotional framework. Loss is emotional, not intellectual. We feel loss before we understand it.

Stay Connected

The feeling of loss can and must be managed for the sake of what will come and in language that matters to others. Continual communication is critical at this stage. The Christian leader will need to stay connected in three vitally important ways.

First, stay connected to the followers. This is not always easy. In fact, it will often require the leader's willingness to set aside a personal sense of urgency to really hear others. People are willing to follow, to make necessary changes, when they have a leader who is with them—not always out in front of them.

Some leaders think of this as the "hand-holding stage," but it is so much more than that. This is the time for building the currency of trust in our leadership bank. This is when the Christian practices what the Savior preached, through compassionate and purposive presence. The energy for change will build invisibly in this stage.

Second, stay connected with your mission. Remember the change and the reasons it is necessary. Be present to those who are letting go of the past for the sake of a future they cannot yet see. Remind them that it is coming and that you want them to participate in it. This is the time for vividly painting the vision for the future. Again, the leader must use language that matters to the hearer . . . not just to himself or herself. The leader needs to know his or her followers well enough to understand, value, and feel comfortable using that language.

Lastly, the leader must stay connected to God in Jesus Christ. As has been said previously, effective leaders are first followers. The art of followership provides the inner strength for the patience and purpose that persistence requires. The leader cannot compromise his or her commitment to necessary change, but neither can he or she lose sight of those values that underlie the mission of the Christian church. When followers sense this inner commitment on the part of the leader, they are much more willing to make the changes necessary.

Is Change Good or Bad?

In this communication stage of managing change, the health of the change itself is challenged. This is necessary for two reasons. First, not all change is good. Some change leads to greater disease. Some visions are pipe dreams. Testing the vision and the change empowers the leader with the followers to discern whether or not this change is good.

Second, such challenges are good because they refine the change and the vision. No one can know all the outcomes of any change. The law of unintended consequences suggests that often the most dramatic outcomes of change are total surprises. When President Lyndon Johnson created the Great Society and developed a system for welfare that would lift persons from poverty, he did not intend to create generation after generation of dependents on federal subsidy. Similarly, when the engineers at 3M were developing a malleable glue, they didn't intend to develop "Post-it" notes.

More than anticipating unintended consequences, this stage of managing change invites others to own the need for change as well as the vision for its outcome. This ownership enlists others in the process for change and creates the momentum discussed in chapter 4.

As the communication process occurs, the leader should be conscious of creating the tension for change. In anticipating the implementing of change, let the leader enlist at least one curmudgeon, a person who resists change but is willing to pursue it when the need becomes clear. When the tension for change requires someone to speak to those who are still holding back, this curmudgeon is the one to do it.

Others should also be enlisted in a transition team, a group of disciples who represent those who catch the vision first, second, and last. This team's commitment to creating a vital, mission-driven church must be clear and steadfast. These are persons who understand what is and hope for what can be, even though both are necessarily vague at times. Their qualifications are simple: they must be credible, engaged persons who bring a value for the past with a clarity about what the future must include.

John Kotter has said that leaders undercommunicate by a factor of ten.[3] This is the stage for the leader and the transition team to overcommunicate. People should get tired of the messages. They should know the burning platform, the changes coming, and the hoped-for outcomes like the verses of an old hymn . . . or, better yet, like the words of a praise song that are simple and repetitive. Here we *make haste slowly*. The key is planned redundancy.

Celebrate the Advances

"At Prince of Peace, we care more about your soul than your pocketbook," I said in worship that Sunday. "But because we care about your soul, we are going to talk about your pocketbook."

This was not a Sunday for a classic stewardship or tithing sermon. The scripture text, however, was clear: Jesus said, "Do not store up for yourselves treasures on earth, where moth and rust consume and where thieves break in and steal; but store up for yourselves treasures in heaven, where neither moth nor rust consumes and where thieves do not break in and steal" (Matthew 6:19-20). This was an opportunity to call for a discipleship that took seriously the words of the Savior. The question was whether, as followers of Jesus Christ, we were laying up treasures only on earth or in eternity as well. And the opportunity was given for me to celebrate another fact: "Did you know that those who have become a part of

Prince of Peace through our Discipleship Connections course are giving at a rate 25 percent above others?" I asked. "The point I am making," I continued, "is that those who catch sight of the joy of discipleship understand the joy and discipline of giving. That's what I'd like to invite you all into."

This is a celebration of the advances of change. The change at Prince of Peace was to move to discipleship as our basic understanding and framework for ministry and mission. One clear advance was that those who embraced the vision were giving more, and more often. This celebration became an opportunity to challenge or invite others into the vision for the change.

Along with celebrating the advances, it helps to celebrate the past. When one of our great leaders of the past died, his funeral was a celebration of the best of our past. This was a man who had a zeal for evangelism, a heart for the church, and a life of discipleship. Before hundreds, his family lifted up his life. And as presiding minister at his funeral, I had the great privilege of affirming that his work continues in our commitments today. The bridge between the past and the future was clearly identified in that present moment. Others made the connection and told me about it at the reception later.

The leader makes this bridge a reality as she or he manages key change in the organization we call the church. The script is real and, we hope, genuine. Speaking to a group of new disciples, I said, "Who we have been has made possible who we are; and who we are today will make possible who we will be tomorrow. The changes before us are necessary, but we have received much from our past that makes this jump into the waters of the future possible. We will move into the future God has prepared for us. We deeply desire you to join us."

Be Opportunistic, then Strategic

Such a script will make possible the identifying and seizing of opportunities that could not have been anticipated. The death of this beloved leader of the church could not have been anticipated, but it presented a real opportunity for advancing the vision for our ministry and mission because it was so consistent with his life and passion. The opportunity became strategic.

Strategic planning is a good thing if, once it has been developed, the plan is not slavishly followed. The real power of strategic planning is not in its ability to predict the future but in its clarity of where we are and have come from. There is much evidence to suggest that strategic planning hinders rather than helps organizations. My observation is that churches that do strategic planning are helped by the purposive process more than by the predicted outcomes. The future is unknown. Strategies to move us more effectively into the future work best when we see them as positioning us for unknown opportunities. When the opportunity becomes visible and it fits with the vision and mission, then the strategy ought to free the church to seize the day!

If leadership is like a dance, as has already been suggested, then a strategic plan is like a floor chart of the dance steps. When we slavishly follow the chart, we may be learning . . . but we aren't dancing yet.

Afterword

This book has suggested that the looping of DNA provides a metaphor or model for creative thinking in the church and helps us understand some of the critical movements in our time and world. Beneath all of this is a passion for the growth of Christ's church. The church of Jesus the Savior has been created in the power of the Holy Spirit not for its own sake but for the sake of the world that God loves. The burning platform for us is the inability of so many of our ministries to be effective in mission and ministry in their context.

Rather than experience this as a rejection of the gospel by our world, we can see this as a great opportunity to reform and renew the language and forms of our work. As disciples, we are called to protect and preserve the essentials of the Savior we follow. The difficulty has always been how to do that while being open to the power of the Holy Spirit, who is constantly changing things . . . including the church.

Notes

Chapter 1

1. Michael Michalko, "Thinking like a Genius," in *Exploring Your Future*, ed. Edward Cornish (Bethesda, Md.: World Future Society, 1996), 126 (italics mine).

2. James Gilmore and Joseph Pine, *The Experience Economy* (Boston: Harvard Business School Press, 1999).

3. James Gilmore and Joseph Pine, address at "Exploring off the Map," a Leadership Network Event, May 2000, Denver, Colorado.

4. George Gallup Jr. and D. Michael Lindsay, *Surveying the Religious Landscape* (Harrisburg, Pa.: Morehouse, 1999), 21.

5. Ibid., 22.

6. Ibid., 43.

7. Tom Sine, at a conference hosted by Prince of Peace, May 1995, Burnsville, Minnesota.

8. Jim Collins, address at Leadership Network conference, May 1997, Denver, Colorado.

9. Dietrich Bonhoeffer, *Discipleship,* Dietrich Bonhoeffer Works (Minneapolis: Fortress Press, 2001).

10. Edgar H. Schein, *The Corporate Culture Survival Guide* (San Francisco: Jossey-Bass, 1999), 24.

11. Schein, *The Corporate Culture Survival Guide,* 14.

12. Roger Finke and Rodney Stark, *The Churching of America 1776–1990* (New Brunswick, N.J.: Rutgers University Press, 1992), 1 (italics mine).

Chapter 2

1. Dave Travis, ed., *Explorer Lite,* an e-publication of the Leadership Network, November 3, 2000 (italics mine).

2. Peter M. Senge et al., *The Fifth Discipline Fieldbook : Strategies and Tools for Building a Learning Organization* (New York: Doubleday, 1994), 49.

Chapter 3

1. David Messner, CEO, Park Nicollet Health Care, from address at the conference "*Next*Church," October 14, 2000, Wooddale Church, Eden Prairie, Minnesota.
2. Alan Klass, interview at Mission Growth Ministries, Smithville, Missouri, May 5, 2000.
3. Leonard Sweet, personal conversation, June 2001.
4. Lyle Schaller, from address at the conference "*Next*Church," October 14, 2000, Wooddale Church, Eden Prairie, Minnesota.

Chapter 4

1. Jim Collins, address at Leadership Network conference, May 1997, Denver, Colorado.

Chapter 5

1. Margaret Wheatley, Exploring Off the Map conference, May 2000, Denver, Colorado.

Chapter 7

1. Dr. Mark Zipper, presentation, Prince of Peace Lutheran Church, Burnsville, Minnesota, November 1999.
2. Report to the Evangelical Lutheran Church in America Assembly, August 2001.
3. John P. Kotter, *Leading Change* (Boston: Harvard Business School Press, 1996.